StuffeD

PAGE STREET
PUBLISHING CO.

First published in 2014 by

Page Street Publishing Co.

27 Congress Street, Suite 103

Salem, MA 01970

www.pagestreetpublishing.com

Distributed by Macmillan; sales in Canada by The Canadian Manda Group; distribution in Canada by The Jaguar Book Group.

17 16 15 14   1 2 3 4 5

ISBN-13: 978-1-62414-011-2

ISBN-10: 1-62414-011-4

Library of Congress Control Number: 2013943254

Cover and book design by Page Street Publishing Co.

Photography by Ken Goodman Photography

Food styling by Meg Jones Wall

Printed and bound in China

Page Street is proud to be a member of 1% for the Planet. Members donate one percent of their sales to one or more of the over 1,500 environmental and sustainability charities across the globe that participate in this program.

StuffeD

THE ULTIMATE COMFORT FOOD COOKBOOK

TAKING YOUR Favorite FOODS AND Stuffing THEM TO MAKE NEW, DifferenT AND Delicious MEALS

Dan Whalen

FOUNDER OF THEFOODINMYBEARD.COM

PAGE STREET
PUBLISHING CO.

CONTENTS

Introduction

"You are totally mad, but it's fantastic."

I will never know exactly how I became the mad scientist of comfort food, but when you stuff a full-size cheeseburger into ravioli and serve it on a bun, people start calling you names.

I'm not a culinary trained chef, but I have cooked almost every day for about seven years. I'm not a world traveler, but I've done hours of research to ensure my recipes are rooted in authenticity.

Although in those formative years I may not have learned to cook, I sure did learn how to eat. My mom's side of the family is Italian, and when it comes to eating, they are the best. Throughout my youth I learned to eat spaghetti, manicotti and lasagna. I excelled at eating pasta fagioli, tortellini and chicken Parm.

Upon arrival at college, I was on my own and began to teach myself to cook. I started watching cooking shows and reading the cookbooks written by some of my favorite TV personalities. I was getting the hang of some basic techniques and flavor combinations. The more I learned, the more I wanted to learn. With every step that I could drill down and master, my food became more homemade and, concurrently, more tasty.

I was cooking four or five new recipes each week and after about a year of this I started to develop recipes on my own. It happened that around this time I was trying to learn some new software for my day job in the IT field. I decided to test out my new software skills by creating my own blog. I had something to share. There was a void in the food web that I could fill. This is how The Food in My Beard was born.

Today, I am the chef for a small, independently owned burrito shop, Cafe Burrito, in Boston, for which I created the menu. I am a freelance food writer for General Mills, and of course I still have my blog, thefoodin mybeard.com, which I update with new recipes about four times a week. Although the site may have begun as a way to simply chronicle my cooking and learn some new software, it became something much bigger.

Writing a cookbook has always been something I aspired to do, and over the past two years it is has become a priority. I knew I wanted to do something unique that reflected my creative modern comfort style of cooking, and once I came up with the theme of stuffed foods, the book really started to come together.

For your browsing pleasure, I have included a heat and pig-out scale for each recipe. This should help you quickly find a recipe that suits your current needs for different levels of heat and overall gluttony. For the heat scale, once you hit around 6, things start getting really hot, and anything above 8 . . . only serious pepper heads need apply! Now, let's get to the good stuff!

i. Toasted breadcrumbs

ii. Tabasco Sauce

iii. Shredded chicken

iv. Flour

v. Eggs

CHAPTER 1:

StuffeD Breads

Well before I started seriously cooking, when I was just a college student trying to make my way to success in computer science, there were pretty much two go-to recipes I had in my back pocket. The first one was tacos for dinner, and the other was pepperoni bread. Pepperoni bread was the one that I would pull out to serve as a snack at parties or trips to the beach with my friends. My mom had shown me how easy and delicious it was to make, and from that moment on I made it any chance I got. It was one of the first things that made me feel like cooking wasn't just some chore, but rather a labor of love, and that if you paid just enough special attention to what you were making it would come out all that much better and your friends would love you for it.

People have been stuffing breads with various cheeses, veggies and meats for just as long as bread has existed. In this chapter you will find recipes with pizza dough, puff pastry, cornbread, and even pretzel dough! Fry, bake and steam your way to stuffed bread perfection, whether it be as an appetizer or a side, or for breakfast, lunch or dinner.

Pepperoni Bread

½ batch homemade Pizza Dough (page 194) or 1 package refrigerated or frozen pizza dough

8 ounces (225 g) mozzarella cheese, shredded

2 ounces (56 g) Pecorino Romano cheese, grated

4 ounces (112 g) pepperoni

Simple Marinara (page 194), for serving

This is a super simple recipe that I have been making regularly for years. Well before I even started blogging or became interested in cooking I was making this. It's the best thing you can bring to a party, and it's pretty versatile in that once you get the method down you can stuff it with a variety of fillings.

• •

STUFF IT!: On a floured surface, roll out your pizza dough into a very thin rectangle shape. It should come out to about 15 inches by 12 inches (38 by 30.5 cm). Lay out a layer of cheeses, followed by the pepperoni, then the rest of the cheeses, reserving a small amount. Roll up the dough fairly tight to form a spiral of dough and meat. You should be rolling it the short way, so that it is still 15 inches (38 cm) long after being rolled. Fold the ends of the bread under the roll. Put the roll onto a baking sheet and top with the remaining cheese.

COOK IT: Preheat the oven to 350°F (180°C, or gas mark 4). Bake the bread for about 35 minutes, until nicely browned on top and cooked through. Allow to cool for about 10 minutes, then slice into thin slices. Serve with the Simple Marinara as a dipping sauce.

Aloo Gobi Samosas

MAKES: 6 VERY LARGE SAMOSAS
OR 12 TO 15 SMALL ONES
HEAT: 4.1
PIG-OUT SCALE: 4.3

SAMOSA DOUGH

1½ cups (180 g) flour

2 tablespoons (30 ml) vegetable oil

¼ to ½ cup (60 to 120 ml) cold water

ALOO GOBI

2 Yukon gold potatoes, chopped into bite-size chunks

½ head cauliflower, chopped into bite-size chunks

3 tablespoons (42 g) butter

Salt

1 tablespoon (6 g) curry powder, homemade (page 191) or store-bought

1 onion, diced

1 teaspoon cumin seed

1 tablespoon (15 ml) oil

3 cloves garlic, grated

1-inch (2.5-cm) piece ginger, grated

3 Thai chiles, diced, seeds removed if desired

¼ cup (16 g) chopped cilantro stems

1 (14½-ounce [406-g]) can tomatoes

¾ cup (112 g) peas

¼ cup (16 g) chopped cilantro leaves

Indian samosas and South American empanadas are pretty similar if you think about it. They use a pastry dough that is made up of mostly flour with a little bit of fat, they can be baked but taste a little better fried, and of course, there are endless possibilities for filling options. The following recipes can be mixed and matched depending on whether you prefer the empanada or samosa wrap better. Aloo gobi samosas are a fairly common Indian variety, but the ones you make fresh at home are ten times better than the ones that have been sitting out at the Indian grocery all day.

• •

MAKE THE DOUGH: Mix the flour and oil in a bowl. With your fingers, work the oil into the flour. You will notice that there will be clumps of flour where the oil has collected. Work these clumps with your fingers to evenly distribute. Finally, add the water, starting with the minimal amount listed, and only adding just enough to bring the dough together as you stir and mix with a fork. Once it comes together, begin kneading with your hands for about 5 minutes. Wrap the dough in plastic and refrigerate for at least 15 minutes while you prep the rest of the ingredients.

MAKE THE FILLING: Preheat the oven to 450°F (230°C, or gas mark 8).

Put your chopped potato and cauliflower into two separate bowls. Melt the butter and add salt to taste and half of the curry powder to the butter. Split the butter mixture into the two separate bowls of veggies and toss to coat. Place the veggies on two baking pans. Put the potatoes into the oven for about 7 minutes, and then add the cauliflower. When everything is browned and tender, take the veggies out of the oven, about 15 minutes total for the potatoes and 8 for the cauliflower.

Mix the grated garlic and ginger together and add the diced chiles to the mixture. Cook the onion and cumin seed in the oil until the onions are browned, 6 to 8 minutes. Add the ginger-garlic-chile paste and the cilantro stems and cook 2 minutes. Add the other half of your curry powder, cook 1 minute. Add the tomatoes and cook for about 5 minutes, allowing a lot of the tomato liquid to absorb. Taste and add salt if needed. Add the peas and cook until heated through, 3 to 4 minutes. Add the roasted potato and cauliflower and toss to coat. The mixture should be fairly thick and dry at this point, so that you are able to stuff it into the pastry, so if it isn't, let it simmer a little longer. Remove from the heat and stir in the cilantro leaves.

STUFF IT!: Split the dough into 3 balls and roll out each ball into rounds about ⅛ inch (3 mm) thick. Cut the round equally through the center. Take the half circle in your hand and fold the flat end onto itself in the middle. Press it together well to seal the seam. Lift it up and you should have a cone shape. Add one-sixth of the slightly cooled aloo gobi mixture into the cone. Fold the rounded edge over and seal to form a cone-shaped treat. Repeat to make the remaining samosas.

COOK IT: You can bake or fry these samosas. Frying is more popular and a bit more delicious, but baking works, too. To fry, heat vegetable oil in a Dutch oven to 350°F (180°C). Gently drop in your samosa and let it cook until browned, about 2 minutes. If you want to bake it, set the oven for 450°F (230°C, or gas mark 8), and lightly brush a baking sheet with oil. Place your samosas on the sheet and cook until browned, about 15 minutes. Keep your eye on them and flip when needed, as the bottom of the samosa will brown faster than the top. Serve with Basil-Carrot Raita dipping sauce (page 195)!

Ginger Peanut Chicken Samosas

A spicier Thai twist on the samosa, these ginger peanut chicken pockets really pack some flavor. As always, remove the seeds from the chiles for a milder version. This recipe uses the same dough and stuffing/cooking methods from pages 12 to 13.

• •

MAKES: 6 LARGE SAMOSAS OR 12 TO 15 SMALL ONES
HEAT: 6.4
PIG-OUT SCALE: 5.2

GINGER CHICKEN FILLING

2 chicken breasts

2 tablespoons (30 ml) olive oil

2-inch (5-cm) piece ginger, grated

3 cloves garlic, grated

3 red chiles, diced, seeds removed if desired

2 tablespoons (30 ml) soy sauce

1 tablespoon (15 ml) Sriracha

1 tablespoon (15 ml) sesame oil

½ cup (55 g) shredded carrot

½ cup (75 g) crushed peanuts

¼ cup (16 g) chopped cilantro

MAKE THE DOUGH: Make the dough following the recipe for Aloo Gobi Samosas (page 12).

MAKE THE FILLING: In a frying pan over medium-high heat, sear the chicken in the olive oil to brown, then cover, reduce the heat to medium and simmer until cooked through, flipping as needed. Meanwhile, split the grated ginger into two separate ramekins. Mix the garlic and chiles into one of the ginger portions. Remove the chicken from the pan and set on a cutting board. Add in a splash more oil if needed, and toss in the garlic, ginger and chile mixture. Sauté for about 2 minutes, then add the soy sauce, Sriracha and sesame oil. Reduce the heat to low. Chop up the chicken into somewhat shredded little ½-inch (1.3-cm) cubes. Add the chicken back to the pan, along with the remaining ginger and the carrot and stir well. Remove from the heat and add the peanuts and cilantro. Allow to cool before stuffing and baking or frying, following the directions on page 13. Serve with Thai Sweet and Sour Sauce (page 195) or Basil-Carrot Raita (page 195) for dipping.

Beef and Broccoli Empanadas

MAKES: 8 EMPANADAS
HEAT: 4.5
PIG-OUT SCALE: 5.6

In Brazil there is a saying, "You are the olive in my empanada." To most Americans that might seem like an odd thing to say, because olives aren't the first thing that comes to mind when we think of empanadas. Once you try an olive in an empanada, though, you will realize that most empanadas are not complete without them, and it brings a lot more weight to the phrase.

• •

EMPANADA DOUGH

1¾ cups (210 g) flour

½ cup (112 g) butter, chopped into ½-inch (1.3-cm) cubes and frozen for 30 minutes

1 egg

⅓ cup (80 ml) water

BEEF AND BROCCOLI FILLING

1 pound (454 g) ground beef

2 tablespoons (30 ml) oil

Salt and pepper

1 onion, diced

2 cloves garlic, minced

2 jalapeños, diced

2 tablespoons (12 g) taco seasoning, homemade (page 192) or store-bought

1 cup (235 ml) beer

1 head broccoli, chopped into ½-inch (1.3-cm) chunks

8 ounces (225 g) Cheddar cheese, grated

½ cup (50 g) chopped olives

EGG WASH

1 egg

¼ cup (60 ml) water

Flour

MAKE THE DOUGH: Mix the flour and butter in a bowl. With your fingers, work the butter into the flour. Then beat the egg into the water and pour the water/egg mixture into the flour and mix with a fork. Once it comes together, begin kneading with your hands. Knead for about 5 minutes, until the dough is smooth. Refrigerate for at least 15 minutes while you prep the rest of the ingredients.

MAKE THE FILLING: In a skillet over high heat, brown the beef in the oil until cooked through, season with salt and pepper, and remove from the pan. Add the onion to the same pan and cook over medium heat to sweat, 4 to 5 minutes. When the onions are just showing signs of browning, add the garlic and jalapeños to the pan, followed by the taco seasoning. Stir well and cook for 1 minute. Add the beer to the pan and scrape the bottom of the pan to get any browned bits incorporated into the sauce. Put the beef back in along with the broccoli. Lightly season with salt and simmer until the broccoli is tender and much of the liquid has evaporated, about 10 minutes. Let the mixture cool, then mix the cheese and olives into the beef.

STUFF IT!: Roll out your empanada dough into 8 thin rounds. Place some of the filling onto the middle of each round. Fold the round over and seal by lightly wetting the edge with your finger. Fold little bits of dough over itself to form that famous empanada look (see picture on page 16).

COOK IT: You can bake or fry these empanadas. To fry, heat vegetable oil in a Dutch oven to 350°F (180°C). Gently drop in your empanada and let it cook until browned, about 2 minutes. If you want to bake it, set the oven for 400°F (200°C, or gas mark 6), and lightly flour a baking sheet. Mix the egg with the water and beat until smooth. Place your empanadas on the sheet and brush nice and evenly with the egg wash. Bake until golden brown, about 30 minutes.

Cuban Sandwich Empanadas

MAKES: 8 SMALL EMPANADAS
HEAT: 0.5
PIG-OUT SCALE: 6.8

Cuban sandwiches are one of my favorite flavor combinations, as you will quickly find out when it appears several times in the pages of this book. It might seem like a grilled ham and cheese isn't that revelatory, but once you add that savory roast pork, juicy pickles and tangy mustard, it really changes the game. These little Cuban sandwich pockets will take your game-day party to the next level.

ROAST PORK FILLING

¾ pound (340 g) boneless country-style pork ribs

¼ cup (60 ml) red wine vinegar

¼ cup (44 g) mustard

2 tablespoons (30 ml) Worcestershire sauce

STUFFING

16 pickle slices

16 Swiss cheese slices

8 ham slices

MAKE THE DOUGH: Make the dough following the recipe for Beef and Broccoli Empanadas (page 15).

MAKE THE FILLING: Preheat the oven to 300˚F (150˚C, or gas mark 2).

Chop the pork into 1-inch (2.5-cm) cubes. Toss in the vinegar, mustard and Worcestershire sauce. Place in an oven-safe frying pan and cover with foil. Bake for 2½ hours, stirring once halfway through the cooking time. Remove from the oven and shred the pork with the cooking liquid.

STUFF IT!: Roll out your empanada dough into 8 thin rounds. Place one-eighth of the pork filling, 2 pickle slices, 2 cheese slices and 1 ham slice on each round. Fold the round over and seal by lightly wetting the edge with your finger. Fold little bits of dough over itself to form that famous empanada look (see picture on page 16). Cook following the directions on page 15.

Chicken Stuffed Waffles

MAKES: 8 WAFFLES
HEAT: 1.3
PIG-OUT SCALE: 7.1

Chicken and waffles was the craze of the moment a few years back, and now it has leveled out as a comfort food staple. Eating perfect fried chicken in concert with perfect waffles is a delicious treat, but putting the chicken right inside the waffles is a fun twist that your friends will never expect! Instead of doing all the work of frying the chicken just to put it into the waffles, we can get the flavor profile of fried chicken with a few unexpected additions to the waffle batter.

FILLING

1 pound (454 g) chicken tenders
Salt and pepper
Oil
½ cup (60 g) panko breadcrumbs

WAFFLE BATTER

1 cup (120 g) flour
⅓ cup (40 g) cornstarch
½ teaspoon baking powder
¼ teaspoon baking soda
½ teaspoon salt
1 teaspoon sugar
1½ cups (355 ml) buttermilk
⅓ cup (75 g) unsalted butter, melted
1 egg
1 tablespoon (15 ml) Tabasco sauce

Maple syrup, for serving

MAKE THE FILLING: Season the chicken with salt and pepper and sear in a hot pan with a splash of oil. Cover and turn the heat down to low. Cook for about 10 minutes, until cooked through. Remove from the heat. Roughly chop half the chicken and shred the other half.

Lightly toss the breadcrumbs with 1 tablespoon (15 ml) or more of oil. Spread on a baking sheet and broil until browned, about 3 to 5 minutes. Watch closely and stir once during cooking so everything can toast evenly without burning.

MAKE THE WAFFLE BATTER: Mix all the waffle ingredients in a large bowl, starting with the dry ones, followed by the wet ones. Whisk to combine, but don't worry about it getting fully incorporated. There will be lumps.

STUFF IT!: Fold the chicken and breadcrumbs into the waffle batter.

COOK IT: Preheat the waffle iron. Ladle the waffle batter into the waffle iron and cook according to the manufacturer's instructions. Serve with maple syrup.

French Toast Three Ways

MAKES: 6 LARGE SLICES
OF FRENCH TOAST
HEAT: 0
PIG-OUT SCALE: 4.4

As a kid French toast was my go-to breakfast item on any menu, but these days I find I almost never order it. What happened? Unfortunately, over the past ten years, I think I've eaten so many bad versions that they may have scared me. They're either too sweet, too thin, or too classy. In my opinion, a good French toast should be simple. I use a nice crusty ciabatta, soak it in egg for a bit, stuff it with deliciousness, and toss it into a frying pan for a few minutes. These three simple stuffed French toast recipes are my response to bad French toast everywhere.

• •

Egg in a French Toast Cave

1 crusty ciabatta loaf (about 18 inches [46 cm] long)

6 egg yolks

SOAKING LIQUID
5 eggs
¼ cup (60 ml) milk
Pinch of salt
Pinch of pepper
Pinch of sugar

Butter and oil, for frying

PREPARE THE BREAD: Cut your ciabatta into 6 equal pieces. Cut a cavity into each piece of the bread from a surface that isn't covered with crust. Cut the piece of bread you have removed into a 1-inch (2.5-cm) "lid" that can be returned to the bread as a cover.

MAKE THE SOAKING LIQUID: Combine all the ingredients in a large bowl. Add the bread and soak for about 10 minutes, then flip the slices and soak another 10 minutes.

STUFF IT!: Drop an egg yolk into each bread cavity and cover with the reserved piece of bread.

COOK IT: In a large skillet, gently fry the bread in a little butter and oil over medium heat, flipping a few times to make sure each piece cooks on all surfaces.

Tomato Basil Stuffed French Toast

1 crusty ciabatta loaf (about 18 inches [46 cm] long)

2 balls fresh mozzarella, each sliced into 6 pieces

12 basil leaves

1 ripe tomato, cut into 6 slices

Salt

SOAKING LIQUID

5 eggs

¼ cup (60 ml) milk

Pinch of salt

Pinch of pepper

Pinch of sugar

Butter and oil, for frying

STUFF IT!: Cut your ciabatta into 6 equal pieces. Choose one of the crusted edges of each piece, and make a small slit into the bread. Make mini stacks starting with some mozzarella, then a basil leaf, a tomato slice, another basil leaf, and then another piece of mozzarella. Be sure to lightly salt the tomato and also the cheese if it tastes bland. Stuff your mozzarella sandwich into the small slit in the bread. It will be a tight fit, but you can do it!

MAKE THE SOAKING LIQUID: Combine all the ingredients in a large bowl. Add the stuffed bread and soak for about 10 minutes, then flip the slices and soak another 10 minutes.

COOK IT: In a large skillet, gently fry the bread in a little butter and oil over medium heat, flipping a few times to make sure each piece cooks on all surfaces.

Ricotta Nutella Stuffed French Toast

1 crusty ciabatta loaf (about 18 inches [46 cm] long) or if you want to get a bit more decadent with it, go with a brioche

1 cup (250 g) ricotta

½ cup (125 g) Nutella

SOAKING LIQUID

5 eggs

¼ cup (60 ml) milk

Pinch of salt

Pinch of pepper

Pinch of sugar

Butter and oil, for frying

STUFF IT!: Cut the bread into 6 equal pieces (or if using brioche, into 2-inch [5-cm] slices). Make a slit on one of the crust edges. Mix the ricotta and Nutella together in a small bowl. With a piping bag (or just a zip-top bag with a hole cut in the corner), pipe the ricotta mixture into the bread, splitting it evenly among the 6 slices.

MAKE THE SOAKING LIQUID: Combine all the ingredients in a large bowl. Add the stuffed bread and soak for about 10 minutes, then flip the slices and soak another 10 minutes.

COOK IT: In a large skillet, gently fry the bread in a little butter and oil over medium heat, flipping a few times to make sure each piece cooks on all surfaces.

Epic Timpano

CHICKEN PARM

1 cup (115 g) breadcrumbs

1 cup (100 g) grated Parmesan cheese

½ cup (32 g) fresh chopped parsley

2 cups (240 g) flour

Salt

3 eggs

Olive oil, for frying

1 pound (454 g) boneless, skinless chicken breast

PASTA

1 pound (454 g) ziti

1½ pounds (680 g) spaghetti

2 cups (470 ml) Cream Sauce (page 195)

1 quart (940 ml) Simple Marinara (page 194)

2 (17.3-ounce [484-g]) packages puff pastry

1 pound (454 g) Italian sausage

1 pound (454 g) meatballs (page 110)

¼ pound (113 g) provolone, grated

This recipe is an absolute masterpiece of overindulgence. Every time I have eaten this, I couldn't move for the rest of the evening. It's just too good to stop eating! Don't make it if you have plans afterward, and reserve it for special occasions.

• •

MAKE THE CHICKEN PARM: Mix the breadcrumbs, Parm and parsley in a shallow bowl. Put the flour in another with a pinch of salt. In the third, whisk the eggs. In a frying pan, heat up about a ¼ inch (6 mm) olive oil. Slice the chicken breasts the long way to make them thinner. Use a mallet or other blunt object in your kitchen to pound out the breasts. While doing this, cover the chicken with plastic wrap so as not to get chicken splatter all over the kitchen. Once the chicken is pounded out, lightly dredge in the flour, followed by the egg and then finally the breadcrumb mixture. Press hard to adhere the breading to the chicken. Brown the chicken on both sides, about 5 minutes per side. Lightly season with salt and set aside on paper towels to dry.

PREPARE THE PASTAS: Boil the ziti separately from the spaghetti. Immediately mix the ziti with the cream sauce, and do the same with the spaghetti and marinara. Don't use all of the sauces, because you don't want the inside of the timpano to be super wet, or else it will just fall apart when you cut it. Reserve some of the sauces to serve on the side.

BUILD IT!: On your workspace, lay out 2 sheets of the puff pastry next to each other, slightly overlapping, and roll them out so they become one large sheet. Grease the biggest oven-safe bowl you have and then lay your puff pastry down. Begin with the cream sauced ziti at the bottom of the bowl (this will be the top later). Next, add a layer of sausage, then some spaghetti, then meatballs, then more spaghetti, followed by a layer of provolone, then the chicken Parm at the top (which will be the bottom).

COOK IT: Preheat the oven to 375°F (190°C, or gas mark 5). Get the monstrosity into the oven and bake it for about 1 hour and 15 minutes.

THE MOMENT OF TRUTH: Let the timpano sit for AT LEAST 15 minutes, if not closer to 25. Put a nice sturdy baking sheet or a cutting board on top of the bowl. Grab the bowl and the cutting board, holding them together tightly, and flip the whole thing. Put it on the table and slowly and gently lift the bowl off the timpano, giving it gentle nudges and shakes if needed. Present the timpano to your guests and let them bask in its glory before finally slicing it, passing out the pieces, and then inevitably taking a nap.

Cheeseburger Slider Steamed Buns

BUN DOUGH

2¼ teaspoons active dry yeast

1 cup (235 ml) warm water

4½ cups (540 g) flour

¼ cup (50 g) sugar

½ cup (120 ml) hot water

2 tablespoons (30 ml) vegetable oil

BURGER FILLING

1 pound (454 g) ground beef

2 large onions, diced

2 tablespoons (28 g) unsalted butter

5 slices American cheese, each cut into 4 pieces

Ketchup, for serving

Did you know that true sliders are steamed and not grilled? That's what makes them so juicy and delicious. They are placed on a bed of sautéing onions, and the steam from the onions cooks the burgers. This made me think, why not steam the burger right inside the bun? Why not incorporate Asian-style steamed buns into this process, cooking the bread AND the meat at the same time? Well, ask no further! This recipe is easier than it seems, very cheap and over-the-top delicious.

• •

MAKE THE DOUGH: Mix the yeast, warm water and 1 cup (120 g) of the flour in a medium bowl and let sit for 1 hour until bubbles form. Mix the sugar with the hot water and oil in a small bowl. Add this to the yeast mixture along with the remaining 3½ cups (420 g) flour and knead until smooth, about 12 minutes. Cover and let rise for 1 hour.

MAKE THE FILLING: Form the beef into 20 small patties. In a skillet, sauté the onions in the butter over medium heat until they are deeply browned, about 15 minutes.

STUFF IT!: Divide the dough into 20 uniform pieces. Roll out each piece to ⅛ inch (3 mm) thick, place a patty on it, top with the onions and a slice of cheese and wrap fully with the dough. Repeat to complete all 20 buns.

COOK IT: Steam in batches of 5 or 10 depending on how big your steamer is. Steam over high heat for about 12 to 15 minutes, until cooked through. Serve with ketchup.

Pork Belly Buns

MAKES: 20 LARGE BUNS
HEAT: 4
PIG-OUT SCALE: 7.6

This is the recipe that started the love affair I have with steamed buns. Tender savory pork belly, fluffy pillowy dough and crunchy fresh slaw—it's like an Asian version of a pulled pork sandwich! Sometimes to make it a little easier, I just flatten out some of the dough, steam it and use it to make mini pork bun sliders, but nothing beats the fully wrapped version.

1 batch Bun Dough (page 24)

PORK FILLING
1 pound (454 g) pork belly
3 cloves garlic, grated
½ cup (120 ml) rice wine vinegar
¼ cup (60 ml) Sriracha
¼ cup (60 g) packed brown sugar
¼ cup (60 ml) soy sauce
Salt and pepper

SLAW
2 carrots
¼ head purple cabbage
1 handful mung beans
2 tablespoons (30 ml) Sriracha
2 tablespoons (30 ml) soy sauce
¼ cup (60 ml) rice vinegar
2 cloves garlic, grated

MAKE THE DOUGH: Make the dough following the recipe for Cheeseburger Slider Steamed Buns (page 24).

MAKE THE FILLING: Preheat the oven to 275°F (140°C, or gas mark 1).

Slice the pork belly into slabs 1 inch (2.5 cm) thick and 2 inches (5 cm) long. Combine the garlic, vinegar, Sriracha, brown sugar and soy sauce in a small bowl. Pour the liquid into an oven-safe frying pan. Place the pork into the pan and season with salt and pepper. Spoon some of the liquid on top of the pork. Bake for 1 hour, flip the pieces of pork and return to the oven. Turn the oven up to 300°F (150°C, or gas mark 2). Bake for 1 hour, then flip the pork again. Bake for 30 minutes longer; the pork should be nicely browned and super tender. Remove from the oven and allow to cool. Chop up the pork belly with a fork to form the filling.

MAKE THE SLAW: Shred the carrots and cabbage very finely. You could use a food processor shredding attachment for this, a box grater, a julienne peeler or just a knife. Mix in the remaining ingredients. Stir well and let sit in the fridge for an hour, stirring occasionally.

STUFF IT!: Roll the dough out to ⅛ inch (3 mm) thick. Cut out rounds, about 3 inches (7.5 cm) in diameter. Place some pork onto each round and top it with a pinch of slaw. Fold up, but instead of folding over like a ravioli, it should be folded like a coin purse, with all the edges meeting at the top and then pressed together. Be sure to squeeze out most of the air.

COOK IT: Preheat your steamer and steam the buns in batches of 5 to 10 for about 8 to 10 minutes, until the dough has fully cooked. Serve with the remaining slaw.

Buffalo Chicken Buns

MAKES: 20 LARGE BUNS
HEAT: 7.5
PIG-OUT SCALE: 6.3

Continuing with the idea of putting American bar food into Asian-style steamed buns, our next subject is buffalo chicken. We already know buffalo chicken works great with bread in things like sandwiches and calzones, so why not in steamed buns? The delicious buffalo sauce seasons the dough, and these buns come out moist and flavorful.

• •

1 batch Bun Dough (page 24)

BUFFALO CHICKEN FILLING

¼ cup (56 g) unsalted butter

1 pound (454 g) boneless, skinless chicken thighs

2 cloves garlic, grated

1 habanero pepper, minced

1 teaspoon red pepper flakes

½ cup (120 ml) cayenne sauce

½ cup (65 g) diced carrot

½ cup (60 g) diced celery

Salt

1 tablespoon (20 g) honey

Blue cheese or ranch dressing, for serving

MAKE THE DOUGH: Make the dough following the recipe for Cheeseburger Slider Steamed Buns (page 24).

MAKE THE FILLING: In a frying pan over medium heat, melt the butter and throw in the chicken. Cook for about 10 minutes, until lightly browned. Add the garlic, habanero and red pepper flakes and mix well. Add the cayenne sauce and honey and continue to simmer for another 10 to 15 minutes, until the chicken is very tender. Shred and break up the chicken right there in the pan with a wooden spoon. Remove from the heat and stir in the carrot and celery. Taste and add more red pepper flakes if you want it spicier. Season with salt if needed, but depending on the brand and type of butter and cayenne sauce you are using, it may be salty enough.

STUFF IT!: Divide the dough into 20 uniform pieces. Roll out the dough to ⅛ inch (3 mm) thick, place a few tablespoons of the chicken onto the dough and wrap fully. Repeat to complete all 20 buns.

COOK IT: Steam in batches of 5 or 10 depending on how big your steamer is. Steam over high heat for about 12 to 15 minutes, until cooked through. Serve with some blue cheese or ranch dressing for dipping.

Sweet Potato Tamales

MAKES: 8 TAMALES
HEAT: 2.3
PIG-OUT SCALE: 4.1

TAMALE DOUGH

3 large sweet potatoes

Vegetable oil, for coating potatoes

2 teaspoons salt, plus more for sprinkling on potatoes

Pepper

6 tablespoons (84 g) butter, at room temperature

Pinch of ground cloves

Pinch of cinnamon

1½ cups (180 g) masa harina

1 cup (235 ml) water

BEEF FILLING

1 pound (454 g) ground beef

Salt

1 onion, diced

1 bell pepper, diced

3 cloves garlic, minced

1 tablespoon (6 g) cumin

¼ cup (60 ml) chipotle sauce

1 cup (235 ml) water

2 tablespoons (40 g) honey

8 cornhusks

8 ounces (225 g) Cheddar cheese

Salsa, guacamole and sour cream, for serving

Tamales are such a fun thing to cook, and the addition of sweet potato to the tamale dough in this recipe really makes things super moist and crazy delicious.

MAKE THE DOUGH: Preheat the oven to 350°F (180°C, or gas mark 4). Coat the sweet potatoes in a little oil, salt and pepper, and place on a baking sheet. Roast until soft and tender, about an hour. Remove the skin from the sweet potatoes and mash them with the butter, salt, cloves and cinnamon. Add in the masa, followed by the water, and mix well. The desired texture is that of a wet peanut butter, so if it is too dry, add a little more water.

MAKE THE FILLING: Season the beef with salt and sauté in a skillet over medium-high heat until browned and cooked through, about 5 to 7 minutes. Remove from the pan. Strain most of the fat until there is just enough to coat the bottom of the pan. In the same pan, cook the onion and pepper until they start to brown around the edges, 10 to 12 minutes. Add the garlic and cook for another minute. Add the beef back to the pan along with the cumin and chipotle, stirring to combine. Splash in the water and scrape all the browned bits off the bottom of the pan and into the sauce. Finally, add the honey and simmer until the water has reduced and a nice sauce has formed.

STUFF IT!: One by one, lay out a cornhusk, spread one-eighth of the tamale dough on it in a rectangle shape and add a small strip of the ground beef filling, followed by some cheese. Roll the tamale so the beef and cheese are fully encased in the dough. Use the husk to wrap it and form a nice tube shape, almost as if you were rolling sushi. (You all know how to expertly roll sushi, right?)

COOK IT: Steam the tamales for an hour and a half. When finished, unwrap and serve with salsa, guac and sour cream, if you like those sorts of things.

Fried Dough Mozzarella Bites

MAKES: ABOUT 40 BITES
HEAT: 0
PIG-OUT SCALE: 5.9

These little guys are one of the most viewed posts of all time on The Food in My Beard, and for good reason! Only problem is when I originally made them, I totally messed up and all the cheese came flying out of the balls while frying. Since then, I fixed up the recipe, and added a few flavor boosters like garlic and oregano to make this a killer dish.

CHEESE FILLING

1 pound (454 g) mozzarella
½ cup (60 g) cornstarch
1 teaspoon garlic powder
1 teaspoon ground oregano
1 teaspoon salt

Flour, for dusting
1 loaf pizza dough, homemade (page 194) or store-bought
Oil, for frying
Simple Marinara (page 194), for dipping

MAKE THE FILLING: The key here is to buy the firmer blocks of mozzarella, and not the fresh kind that floats in water. Chop up the mozzarella into ½-inch (1.3-cm) cubes. Mix the cornstarch with the garlic, oregano and salt and lightly dust the cubes of cheese. Put the cheese into the freezer for at least 30 minutes, but preferably 1 to 2 hours.

STUFF IT!: With a light dusting of flour on your work surface, roll out the dough very thin, about ¼ inch (6 mm) thick. Break off small pieces of dough one by one, and use them to wrap the mozzarella cubes. Have a small cup of water ready, and dip your fingers into the water, using it like glue, to help seal the little dough balls. Roll the balls in your hand to make them uniform, and make sure they are sealed. Dust with flour and set aside until you are ready to fry.

COOK IT: Preheat the oil in a deep skillet to 350°F (180°C). Fry each ball for about 3 to 5 minutes, until browned and cooked, but just before the mozzarella explodes from the dough (you may need to explode a few before you get the hang of the timing). Serve with marinara sauce for dipping.

Meatball Wellington

MAKES: ABOUT 20 SERVINGS
HEAT: 2.0
PIG-OUT SCALE: 6.6

I am always looking for appetizer ideas, and suprisingly my vegetarian aunt came up with this one. Her idea was wrapping each meatball individually, but I thought that was too much work. I made the meatballs into a mini meatloaf and wrapped it similar to an actual beef Wellington, which is normally made with a whole beef tenderloin. Instead of the mushroom paste usually used, I made a tomato sauce that was super thick and pasty.

PASTY TOMATO SAUCE

¼ cup (40 g) diced onion

1 tablespoon (15 ml) olive oil

2 cloves garlic, minced

1 (12-ounce [340-g]) can tomato paste

¼ cup (60 ml) water

1 teaspoon oregano

1 tablespoon Parmesan cheese

Pinch of salt

MEATBALL FILLING

2 cloves garlic

¼ cup (60 ml) milk

3 slices white bread or any leftover bread

1 large egg

½ cup (32 g) chopped parsley

¾ pound (340 g) ground beef

¾ pound (340 g) ground turkey

½ cup (50 g) finely grated Parmesan cheese

1 teaspoon salt

4 ounces (112 g) mozzarella cheese

1 (17.3-ounce [383-g]) package puff pastry

1 egg

MAKE THE TOMATO SAUCE: In a skillet over medium heat, cook the onion in olive oil until it just starts to brown, about 10 minutes. Add the garlic, followed by the tomato paste, and cook for about 3 minutes. Add the water, oregano and cheese. Stir and cook for about 15 minutes and remove from the heat. Season with salt. Allow to cool.

MAKE THE MEATBALL FILLING: Put the garlic into a food processor and pulse to finely chop. Add the milk, bread, egg and parsley to the food processor and process until well combined. It should look like a thick gray paste with flecks of green. In a large bowl, mix the beef and turkey, then add the garlic mixture paste, Parmesan cheese and salt. Mix gently until well combined.

FORM THE LOGS: Split the meat into 2 equal balls. Cut the mozzarella cheese into strips about the size of string cheese. Roll the meat into two long, thin rectangle shapes and place strips of mozzarella cheese on top, almost as if you were about to make a meat sushi roll. Roll the logs of meat around the cheese and seal well. They should only be about 1½ inches (3.8 cm) in diameter. Place on a baking sheet (no need to oil or grease the sheet) and broil on high for about 7 minutes to brown. Roll the meatball logs over and broil another 7 minutes to brown the other side.

STUFF IT!: Thaw your puff pastry according to the package instructions. Lay out a pastry sheet and spread it with some of the tomato sauce. Place the cooled meatball log on top and roll up the pastry around it. Seal it off at the ends. Beat an egg with a splash of water and brush the egg wash mixture onto the pastry.

COOK IT: Preheat the oven to 400°F (200°C, or gas mark 6) and bake the logs for 20 to 25 minutes, until browned. If you see any of the filling leaking, take it out of the oven. Allow your meatball Wellington to cool for about 10 minutes before cutting into 1½-inch (3.8-cm) slices; serve with toothpicks!

Brazilian Cheese Bread (Pao de Queijo) Stuffed with Chorizo

MAKES: ABOUT 20 BALLS
HEAT: 2.0
PIG-OUT SCALE: 5.8

I became familiar with this Brazilian treat after a friend, whose family came from Brazil, took me to some local bakeries. The really awesome thing about these little balls of bread is that they are not only gluten-free, but they also taste incredibly cheesy even though they don't require a ton of the stuff. This twist on the original version sneaks a little chorizo into the bread and has a nice black bean sauce for dipping that is inspired by a Brazilian bean soup.

DOUGH

1 cup (235 ml) milk
½ cup (120 ml) water
1 teaspoon salt
½ cup (120 ml) vegetable oil
3½ cups (420 g) tapioca flour
1 egg
1 cup (100 g) grated Parmesan

CHORIZO FILLING

1 chorizo sausage
Olive oil, for frying

DIPPING SAUCE

1 onion, diced
2 cloves garlic, minced
1 (14-ounce [392-g]) can black beans, drained and rinsed
1 cup (235 ml) chicken stock
Salt and pepper to taste

MAKE THE DOUGH: Bring the milk, water, salt and oil to a very light simmer in a pan over low heat and immediately remove from the heat. Watch it closely because it will boil over easily! Pour it into a mixing bowl and add the flour. Mix well with a spoon instead of a whisk or your hands, as the mixture will get goopy and pasty. Next, mix in the egg and cheese.

MAKE THE FILLING: Chop the chorizo into about twenty ½-inch (1.3-cm) cubes. In a little bit of oil, fry the cubes of chorizo until they are brown and crispy, and render the fat, about 5 to 7 minutes. Remove from the pan and set aside.

MAKE THE SAUCE: Add the onion to the pan of rendered fat and cook for 5 minutes just to sweat. Add the garlic, then the beans and stock. Bring to a simmer and allow to cook for 10 minutes. Remove from the heat. Using an immersion blender, blend the sauce smooth, adding more chicken stock if it's too thick. Season with salt and pepper. Set aside.

STUFF IT!: Form the dough into small balls with your hands nicely coated in flour. Put a chunk of chorizo into the center of each ball and seal. Place on a baking sheet.

COOK IT: Preheat the oven to 350˚F (180˚C, or gas mark 4). Bake the balls for 25 minutes, or until golden and cooked through. Serve with the black bean sauce.

Moroccan Bisteeya Bites

MAKES: 24 POCKETS
HEAT: 0.4
PIG-OUT SCALE: 4.9

Bisteeya is a crazy Moroccan chicken pie that is very sweet, almost to dessert levels. Normally this would be an issue for me, but the flavors are so perfectly balanced that I love it! It is usually a main course, served as slices of a larger pie, or as small individual-size pies, but I like to serve them as little appetizer bites. This recipe will definitely make you remember how good it tastes for years to come.

FILLING

½ teaspoon saffron

2 tablespoons (30 ml) warm water

1 tablespoon (14 g) butter

1 onion, diced

2 cloves garlic, minced

1 inch (2.5 cm) ginger, grated

1½ tablespoons (15 g) ras el hanout, homemade (page 192) or store-bought

2 cups (470 ml) chicken stock

2 pounds (908 g) whole chicken legs

¼ cup (16 g) chopped parsley

Juice of 1 lemon

3 eggs

WRAPPER

½ cup (75 g) toasted almonds

2 tablespoons (25 g) granulated sugar

½ cup (112 g) butter

1 (1-pound [454-g]) package phyllo dough

Confectioners' sugar

Ground cinnamon

MAKE THE FILLING: Mix the saffron with the warm water and let it "bloom" for about 15 minutes. Meanwhile, heat the butter in a heavy-bottomed pot or Dutch oven over medium heat. Add the onion and sauté for about 15 minutes, until lightly browned. Add the garlic, ginger and ras el hanout and cook for 2 minutes. Add the saffron water, chicken stock and chicken legs and simmer for about 35 to 40 minutes, until the chicken is cooked through.

Remove the chicken from the pot, reserving the liquid in the pot, and discard the skin and bones. Shred the chicken and mix it in a bowl with the parsley and lemon juice. Meanwhile, beat the eggs together. Turn the heat up to a strong simmer in the pot, and drizzle the egg into the pot to form ribbons of scrambled egg. Cook for 2 minutes, and then strain, discarding the liquid and adding the egg and onion mixture to the chicken. Mix well.

STUFF IT!: In a food processor, blend the almonds with the granulated sugar to form a crumbly consistency. Do not overprocess or you will have almond butter. Melt the butter and put it into a small bowl with a brush ready to go. Lay the first phyllo sheet on the counter and very lightly brush with the butter. Repeat until you have 3 sheets on top of each other. Sprinkle with the almond mixture.

Cut the sheets into thirds lengthwise, so you have 3 strips of triple-ply phyllo. Put a decent-size scoop of the filling, about ¼ cup (60 g), onto one of the phyllo ends. Fold the filling over diagonally to form a triangle, similar to folding a flag. Keep going until you have gone the whole length of the phyllo and you have a nice wrapped up pie that looks like a fat paper football. Continue rolling sheets of phyllo until you have used all of the filling. Transfer to a baking sheet.

COOK IT: Preheat the oven to 450°F (230 °C, or gas mark 8). Bake the bites for about 15 to 20 minutes. Allow to cool for a few minutes before sprinkling with confectioners' sugar and cinnamon and serving.

Korean Burritos

MAKES: 8 TO 10 BURRITOS
HEAT: 4.2
PIG-OUT SCALE: 3.8

Mixing Korean and Mexican food is a big trend among food trucks in California. I couldn't afford a plane ticket, so I had to take matters into my own hands. I like carnitas burritos, usually made by marinating pork shoulder in a Mexican sauce called mojo before slow roasting it. Applying that same logic to a Korean burrito meant that I marinated my pork shoulder in Korean spices like gochujang and sesame oil. For beans, I went with fresh edamame instead of the standard black or pinto beans. Some kimchi and a fresh salsa with cucumbers and rice vinegar rounded things out.

• •

PORK FILLING

4 pounds (1816 g) pork shoulder
¾ cup (120 g) gochujang
¼ cup (60 ml) sesame oil
¼ cup (60 g) brown sugar
2 tablespoons (30 ml) soy sauce
6 cloves garlic
1 onion, roughly sliced
1 cup (235 ml) water

SALSA

4 large tomatoes
1 onion
4 jalapeños
1 English cucumber
2 tablespoons (30 ml) rice wine vinegar
¼ cup (16 g) chopped cilantro
1 teaspoon salt

RICE

2 cups (330 g) basmati rice
¼ cup (60 ml) sesame oil
2 tablespoons (8 g) chopped cilantro

8 to 10 large flour tortillas
Fresh or frozen edamame, lightly steamed
Kimchi

MAKE THE FILLING: Marinate your pork overnight in the gochujang, sesame oil, brown sugar, and soy sauce. The next morning, add the whole cloves of garlic and roughly sliced onion to a slow cooker. Pour in your pork and marinade and turn it on low for 8 hours. If you don't have a slow cooker, you can roast this in a Dutch oven or deep pot at 250°F (120°C, or gas mark ½) for about 5 hours.

When the pork is done, pull it out and shred it up, removing any overly fatty pieces. Discard the fat from the cooking liquid and add the remaining liquid to the pork. Mash up any remaining solid garlic and onions before adding them to the pork.

MAKE THE SALSA: When the pork is just about done, make your salsa by chopping and combining the salsa ingredients.

MAKE THE RICE: Make the rice by cooking it according to the package instructions, then toss it with the sesame oil and cilantro.

STUFF IT!: Microwave the tortillas between damp paper towels for about 20 seconds to make them pliable (see the sidebar). Add the rice, edamame, kimchi, salsa and pork, and roll it up!

TORTILLA MAGIC

Ever notice how when you go to your favorite burrito shop, the first step is always to place the tortilla into a mysterious box that seems to magically turn a lifeless piece of cardboard into an almost rubbery unbreakable wrap of deliciousness? This is really just a steamer, but it is also what makes the burrito world go 'round. There are a few different ways to steam your tortillas at home to get this same effect and really become a master burrito roller.

1. Most of the time I go with the easiest option, and just microwave the tortilla for about 20 to 25 seconds with a lightly damp paper towel above and below it. While this method doesn't lend itself to the maximum tortilla taste, it does work great in a pinch!

2. Place the tortilla between the two damp paper towels, but this time, put the whole rig into a large plastic zip-top bag. Now when you microwave it, the moisture will stay trapped inside. Try closer to 30 seconds with this method.

3. If you REALLY want to go all out, set up an actual steamer on your stove top. Any steamer will work, from a stand-alone one that you plug in to a bamboo or metal stove top steamer. It doesn't even need to be wider than the actual tortilla, because folding it to steam it isn't an issue. Pop it in there for about 20 to 30 seconds and you're ready to roll.

No matter which method you use, make sure you have aluminum foil ready to wrap your burrito in. It's no coincidence that every single burrito chain uses it! Tightly wrapping your finished burrito with a layer of foil will really seal the deal.

Vietnamese Burritos

MAKES: 6 TO 8 BURRITOS
HEAT: 2.2
PIG-OUT SCALE: 3.2

SALSA

1 English cucumber, diced

2 or 3 fresh vine-ripened tomatoes, diced

15 sprigs mint, finely chopped

1 red onion, diced

2 cloves garlic, grated

1 tablespoon (15 ml) fish sauce

Juice of 2 limes

1 teaspoon salt

GRILLED SKIRT STEAK

¼ cup (60 ml) fish sauce

¼ cup (60 ml) soy sauce

2 tablespoons (30 g) brown sugar

2 tablespoons (30 g) sambol chile paste

2 pounds (908 g) skirt or flank steak

FRIED TOFU

1 (14-ounce [392-g]) package extra-firm tofu

Salt

Vegetable oil

VERMICELLI RICE STICKS

8 ounces (225 g) thin vermicelli rice sticks

2 tablespoons (30 ml) fish sauce

6 to 8 large flour tortillas

Lettuce

Bean sprouts

Peanuts

Sriracha

The Korean burrito is to carnitas as the Vietnamese burrito is to carne asada. This dish takes all the ingredients of a Vietnamese noodle salad called "bun" and wraps it in a flour tortilla. Of all the recipes in this entire book, I think this is the one I crave the most.

• •

MAKE THE SALSA: Combine all of the salsa ingredients in a bowl. Allow to sit for about 30 minutes to allow the flavors to come together.

MAKE THE STEAK: Combine the fish sauce, soy sauce, brown sugar and chile paste in a shallow bowl, add the steak, and marinate in the refrigerator for 30 minutes or up to 12 hours. Grill over high heat for 5 to 7 minutes per side depending on the thickness of the meat. You want it to be a nice medium doneness. Slice your meat thinly against the grain for maximum tenderness.

FRY THE TOFU: Cube your tofu into 1-inch (2.5-cm) squares. Lightly salt the tofu, place on a paper or clean kitchen towel, and allow to dry for at least 1 hour. Coat the bottom of a cast-iron pan or Dutch oven with about ¼ inch (6 mm) of oil and warm over medium heat. Add the tofu and fry on all sides until nicely golden brown. Remove from the pan and season lightly with salt.

COOK THE RICE STICKS: Bring a pot of water to a simmer and remove from the heat. Drop the rice sticks into the hot water. Allow to sit until tender and cooked but not soggy. The time varies by brand, but it could be anywhere from 10 to 30 minutes. Strain and rinse with cold water. Lightly season with fish sauce.

STUFF IT!: Roll up your burrito with the rice noodles first, then tofu, some lettuce, bean sprouts, and peanuts, and finally the meat, salsa and Sriracha.

Cheesesteak Stuffed Soft Pretzel Calzones

MAKES: 4 LARGE CALZONES
HEAT: 2.8
PIG-OUT SCALE: 8.3

I go down to Philly about seven or eight times a year, and what people don't really know about the southeast Pennsylvania area is that cheesesteaks aren't the true regional delicacy; it's actually soft pretzels. In fact, before I started going to Philly, I thought that soft pretzels were nothing more than a dried-out piece of bread rotating in a display case. Soft pretzels from Philly, on the other hand, are a magical moist and chewy, buttery and salty delight. This crazy calzone combines Philly's most iconic food with its true unsung hero.

• •

PRETZEL DOUGH

½ cup (120 ml) warm water

Pinch of sugar

½ (2¼-teaspoon) package active dry yeast

2 cups (240 g) flour, plus more for dusting

1½ teaspoons salt

2 tablespoons (28 g) butter, softened

CHEESESTEAK FILLING

2 or 3 large onions

2 tablespoons (28 g) butter

1 ¼ pounds (568 g) shaved rib eye (any shaved steak will work)

1 cup (135 g) sliced banana peppers

8 ounces (225 g) Monterey Jack, American, or provolone cheese (or a mixture), grated

1 cup (120 g) baking soda, for boiling

1 egg

Coarse or pretzel salt

Simple Marinara sauce (page 194), mustard, or ranch dressing, for serving

MAKE THE DOUGH: Stir the water, sugar, and yeast together in a small bowl and allow to sit for 5 to 10 minutes until it becomes foamy. Meanwhile, mix the flour, salt, and butter in another bowl until well combined (you can use a stand mixer with the dough hook for this portion). Pour the yeast mixture over the flour mixture and stir until incorporated, then begin to knead. Knead for about 7 to 10 minutes, until the dough is no longer sticky and is smooth to the touch, or if using a stand mixer, until it doesn't stick to the sides of the bowl anymore. Put your dough into a clean buttered bowl and cover with a clean towel. Let it rise for 1 hour.

MAKE THE FILLING: Slice the onions into thin ¼-inch (6-mm) round slices. In a frying pan over medium heat, melt the butter and cook the onions until very browned and less than quartered in size, about 40 minutes. Meanwhile, on a cast-iron flat grill or skillet, sear the meat over high heat to brown and cook through. Add the onions and banana peppers to the meat and cook together for about 3 minutes. Remove from the heat and allow to cool. Mix in the cheese.

STUFF IT!: This amount of dough should make 4 large calzones with the meat. If it seems like too much dough, though, feel free to discard however much you need. Split the dough into 4 pieces and roll it out into rounds about ½ inch (1.3 cm) thick. Divide the meat mixture evenly among the rounds. Fold the dough in half to seal the calzone. Roll up the edges decoratively.

BOIL AND BAKE: Bring water to a boil and add the baking soda to it. Also, preheat the oven to 425˚F (220˚C, or gas mark 7).

Beat the egg with a splash of water for an egg wash. One by one, drop the pretzel calzone packets into the boiling water and boil for about 1 minute. Remove from the pot and place right on a baking sheet. When you have boiled all the pretzels, give them all a quick brush with the egg wash and sprinkle with some coarse salt (or pretzel salt if you can find the stuff). Pop in the oven for 15 minutes, until nicely browned and cooked through. Serve with the Simple Marinara or just some mustard or ranch dressing.

Chicken Pretzington

MAKES: 8 CHICKEN PACKETS
HEAT: 0.7
PIG-OUT SCALE: 6.2

PRETZEL DOUGH

1 cup (235 ml) warm water

Pinch of sugar

2¼ teaspoons active dry yeast

4 cups (480 g) flour, plus more for dusting

1 tablespoon (18 g) salt

4 tablespoons (56 g) unsalted butter, softened

CHICKEN FILLING

4 chicken breasts

Salt and pepper

4 ounces (112 g) sharp Cheddar, shredded

½ cup (90 g) honey mustard, plus more for serving

1 cup (120 g) baking soda, for boiling

1 egg

Coarse or pretzel salt

This play on a beef Wellington uses chicken instead of beef, and of course, a soft pretzel in place of puff pastry. It also has honey mustard and cheese, two things that go really well with chicken and pretzels. I originally made this recipe for my family and we totally devoured it in record time.

• •

MAKE THE DOUGH: Stir the water, sugar and yeast together in a small bowl and allow to sit for 5 to 10 minutes until it becomes foamy. Meanwhile, mix the flour, salt and butter in another bowl until well combined (you can use a stand mixer with the dough hook for this portion). Pour the yeast mixture over the flour mixture and stir until incorporated, then begin to knead. Knead for about 7 to 10 minutes, until the dough is no longer sticky and is smooth to the touch, or if using a stand mixer, until it doesn't stick to the sides of the bowl anymore. Put your dough into a clean buttered bowl and cover with a clean towel. Let it rise for 1 hour.

MAKE THE FILLING: Slice the chicken breasts in half the long way. One by one, place a piece of plastic wrap on top of the chicken and pound it out evenly to about ¼ inch (6 mm). Season the meat with salt and pepper and put ½ ounce (14 g) of shredded cheese on top of each piece of chicken. Roll the chicken the long way to form a spiral tube of meat with cheese inside and secure with toothpicks. In a hot frying pan, sear the chicken on all sides. It should be about 75 percent cooked and secure enough to stay rolled up when you remove the toothpicks.

STUFF IT!: Divide the pretzel dough into 8 equal pieces. Roll the dough out into a thin oval shape. Brush about 1 tablespoon (11 g) of mustard onto each dough round. Place a piece of chicken onto the dough perpendicular to the length of the oval. Remove the toothpicks. Roll the dough around the chicken to seal the chicken inside the dough. Pull the ends of the dough to make thin ropes at each end of the chicken. Tie the two ends of the dough into knots.

BOIL AND BAKE: Fill a pasta pot with water and mix in the baking soda. Bring to a boil. Keep an eye on it because it has the tendency to boil over. Also, preheat the oven to 425°F (220°C, or gas mark 7) and grease a baking pan.

Beat the egg with a splash of water for an egg wash. In batches of 2, drop the pretzel packets into the boiling water and boil for about 1 minute. Remove from the pot and place right on the baking pan. When you have done all the pretzels, give them all a quick brush with the egg wash and sprinkle with some coarse salt (or pretzel salt if you can find the stuff). Pop in the oven for about 17 minutes, until nicely browned and cooked through. Use a thermometer to check for doneness if needed. You may need to rotate your pan once during cooking to evenly brown. Serve with extra mustard on the side.

Red Curry Beef Pupusas

MAKES: 5 PUPUSAS
HEAT: 8.5
PIG-OUT SCALE: 6.7

Pupusas are a street food snack originally from Salvador that is basically a thick tortilla stuffed with cheese. This version blends in Thai flavors for a fun and portable twist on red curry. If you can't find Thai basil, feel free to substitute with a 50-50 ratio of Italian basil and mint.

• •

RED CURRY PASTE
(or 2 to 4 tablespoons [22 to 44 g] store-bought)

25 dried red arbol chiles or
2 tablespoons (12 g) Thai or arbol chile powder

10 stalks lemongrass

5 cloves garlic

1-inch (2.5-cm) piece ginger

1 tablespoon (6 g) coriander

1 tablespoon (6 g) cumin

5 shallots

40 Thai basil leaves

1 tablespoon (15 ml) fish sauce

3 tablespoons (45 ml) vegetable oil

BEEF FILLING

1 pound (454 g) ground beef

1 tablespoon (15 ml) vegetable oil

1 cup (235 ml) coconut milk

MASA DOUGH

2 cups (240 g) masa harina

1¾ cups (411 ml) warm water

½ teaspoon salt

Basil-Carrot Raita (page 195), for serving

MAKE THE RED CURRY PASTE: Lightly toast and grind the chiles and spices if applicable. Remove the seeds from the chiles if you want to tone down the spice. Remove the tough outer layers, tops and bottoms of the lemongrass, and dice the tender centers. Put all the ingredients into the food processor and blend into a paste.

MAKE THE FILLING: In a skillet over medium-high heat, sear the meat in the vegetable oil to brown. Strain the fat if there is an excessive amount of it. Add in the curry paste and sauté for about 3 to 5 minutes, stirring often. Add the coconut milk and simmer until most of the liquid evaporates, about 30 minutes.

MAKE THE MASA DOUGH: Mix the ingredients together to form the dough.

STUFF IT!: Divide the dough into 10 equal parts. Roll each piece into rounds about 5½ inches (14 cm) in diameter. Put about 2 heaping tablespoons (30 g) of the curry filling onto 5 of the rounds and spread out evenly. Top with another round and press down well so you have a total of 5 pupusas.

COOK IT: Grill the pupusas on a dry flat grill or frying pan over medium heat for about 8 minutes a side until fully cooked. Serve with some sour cream or the mint raita.

This recipe becomes a bit easier if you substitute store-bought red curry paste. Some brands have a pretty nice flavor, but I just prefer to make it myself because I can get the ingredients cheap and it only takes a few minutes in the food processor.

Pork Belly Stuffed Cornbread Bites

MAKES: 24 MUFFINS
HEAT: 6.1
PIG-OUT SCALE: 7.5

Cornbread and barbecue are a natural pairing, so it only makes sense to put them together. These cornbread muffins are super soft, moist, sweet and go great with the sticky, savory pork belly hidden in the center. It's a classy and neat way to serve what is normally considered messy grub, and if you bring these to your next get-together people will flip out about how good they are.

• •

PORK BELLY FILLING

1¼ pounds (568 g) boneless, skinless pork belly

2 cloves garlic

1½ teaspoons cumin

2 tablespoons (30 g) chipotle peppers in adobo

¼ cup (60 ml) rice wine vinegar

1 tablespoon (11 g) mustard

¼ cup (60 ml) orange juice

¼ cup (60 ml) beer

¼ cup (60 g) brown sugar

Salt and pepper

CORNBREAD BATTER

½ cup (120 g) flour

½ cup (60 g) cornmeal

¼ cup (50 g) sugar

1 teaspoon baking powder

1 teaspoon salt

2 eggs

1½ cups (338 g) sour cream

MAKE THE FILLING: Preheat the oven to 275°F (140°C, or gas mark 1). Slice the pork belly into 24 equal slabs. Chop the garlic, grind the cumin if using whole and take some of the seeds out of the chipotles if you don't like as much heat. Combine the garlic, cumin, chipotles, vinegar, mustard, orange juice, beer and brown sugar in the food processor and process until smooth. Pour the liquid into an oven-safe frying pan. Place the pork into the pan and season with salt and pepper. Spoon some of the liquid on top of the pork. Place the pan into the oven and bake for 1 hour, then flip the pieces of pork, return to the oven, and bake for 1 hour. Flip the pork again and bake for 30 minutes; the pork should be nicely browned and super tender. Remove from the oven and allow to cool. Once cooled, remove the fat from the pan and toss the pork with the cooking liquid to coat.

MAKE THE CORNBREAD BATTER: Grease 24 cups of a mini muffin tin. Mix together the flour, cornmeal, sugar, baking powder and salt in a bowl. In a separate bowl, combine the eggs and sour cream. Add the wet ingredients to the dry and mix well.

STUFF IT!: Divide the batter evenly among the muffin cups and tuck a piece of the pork into each muffin. it doesn't matter if it's sticking out the top slightly.

COOK IT: Preheat the oven to 425°F (220°C, or gas mark 7). Bake for 10 to 12 minutes, until cooked through.

Italian Bolognese Polenta Tamales

MAKES: 8 TO 10 TAMALES
HEAT: 0
PIG-OUT SCALE: 5.2

It dawned on me one day that polenta was very similar to tamale dough. In fact, I usually put cooked cornmeal right in my tamales, so it was a pretty easy connection to make. I took this connection to the logical next step by making a fully Italian version of a tamale with a hearty Bolognese sauce in the center instead of taco meat. At the last minute when I couldn't find cornhusks to wrap the tamales in, I suddenly realized that collard greens would be a perfect wrapper, and that's when the real magic happened.

BOLOGNESE SAUCE

¾ pound (340 g) ground pork
¾ pound (340 g) ground beef
1 onion, diced
4 carrots, diced
3 cloves garlic, minced
6 ounces (168 g) tomato paste
½ cup (120 ml) red wine
1 (28-ounce [784 g]) can crushed tomatoes
1 cup (235 ml) cream
½ cup (50 g) grated Parmesan cheese
1 tablespoon (6 g) oregano
Salt

TAMALES

4 cups (940 ml) chicken stock
1 cup (120 g) cornmeal
1 cup (120 g) masa harina
¼ cup (25 g) grated Parmesan cheese
1 teaspoon cracked black pepper
8 to 10 large collard leaves

MAKE THE SAUCE: In a heavy-bottomed saucepan, brown the meats over high heat. Once fully cooked and nicely browned, remove from the pan. Strain most of the fat until there is just enough to coat the bottom of the pan. Turn the heat down to medium and add the onion and carrot. Cook for about 10 minutes, stirring often, until softened and lightly brown.

Next, the garlic goes in the pan, followed by the tomato paste. Cook the tomato paste for about 3 minutes, stirring constantly. Add the wine and bring to a simmer. Return the meats to the pan along with the crushed tomatoes, cream, Parm and oregano. Taste and add a little salt if needed. Simmer lightly for about 1½ to 2 hours.

MAKE THE TAMALE DOUGH: Bring the chicken stock to a simmer in a saucepot over medium heat. Whisk in the cornmeal and remove from the heat. Stir in the masa, Parm and pepper. Keep stirring as it thickens and it should eventually come to the texture of a thick peanut butter.

STUFF IT!: Remove some of the very thick stem from the center of each collard leaf. Lay a leaf out on your work surface and spread with some of the masa mixture. Top with a scoop of the Bolognese sauce. Roll up the tamale in the leaf, making sure the dough is sealed around the sauce.

COOK IT: Place the tamale into a steamer. Continue to do this until you run out of tamale dough; you should get 8 to 10 tamales. Steam for 45 minutes to 1 hour. Allow to cool for 10 minutes before removing from the steamer and serving.

BBQ Chicken Tamale Enchiladas

MAKES: 8 ENCHILADAS
HEAT: 3.2
PIG-OUT SCALE: 6.4

I originally conceived this idea as a lazy man's tamale, but really, I don't feel comfortable calling something that takes a solid hour and a half "lazy man's" anything. What you can call it, though, is crazy delicious. The soft cornbread batter in the tortillas really combines with the barbecue sauce to make a perfect little pocket of food. The main thing that makes this easier than tamales is that you can bake them instead of steaming them.

CHICKEN FILLING

1 onion

5 jalapeños

4 cloves garlic

1 pound (454 g) boneless, skinless chicken thighs

1 tablespoon vegetable oil

1 tablespoon (6 g) taco seasoning, homemade (page 192) or store-bought

1 cup (260 g) barbecue sauce

½ cup (120 ml) red wine vinegar

TAMALES

½ cup (60 g) yellow cornmeal

½ cup (60 g) masa harina

2 tablespoons (25 g) sugar

1 teaspoon baking powder

1 egg

8 ounces (225 g) sour cream

1 heaping cup (150 g) fresh corn

1 teaspoon salt

8 large flour tortillas

8 ounces (225 g) shredded Chihuahua cheese

MAKE THE FILLING: Dice the onion and jalapeños. Remove the seeds if you want it to be mild. Mince the garlic. In a skillet, brown the chicken thighs on both sides in the oil over medium-high heat, then remove from the pan. Add the onion and jalapeño and sauté for 5 minutes. Add the garlic and cook for 1 minute. Mix in the taco seasoning, followed by the barbecue sauce and vinegar. Mix well and return the chicken to the pan. Allow to simmer for about 20 minutes, until the chicken is cooked through.

Remove the chicken from the pan and chop or shred it. Add a few spoonfuls of the sauce to the chicken and mix it in.

MAKE THE TAMALES: Mix together all of the tamale ingredients in a bowl.

STUFF IT!: Brush some of the extra sauce onto the bottom of a baking pan. Spoon a few tablespoons of the tamale mixture onto a tortilla. Next, add a few tablespoons of chicken to that. Gently roll up the enchilada, folding the ends so the tamale doesn't just leak out everywhere. Put the enchilada into the baking dish and brush more of the sauce onto the tortilla. Repeat with the rest of your tortillas. Your pan should be nicely packed with tamales. Top with any excess sauce, followed by the cheese.

COOK IT: Preheat the oven to 375°F (190°C, or gas mark 5). Bake for 45 minutes to an hour, until the cheese is nicely browned and the tamale mixture is cooked through.

Green Curry Beef Enchiladas

MAKES: 20 SMALL ENCHILADAS
HEAT: 4.2
PIG-OUT SCALE: 3.5

There is a lot of contention in the world of green curry paste recipes online. The problem is that most of them out there are pretty inauthentic. In fact, for every one you find that seems super authentic, you can find a Thai person on another website ranting about how fake it is. This is a green curry paste that I have developed over the years that walks the middle ground between authentic enough that I can feel comfortable about it, American enough that I can find most of the ingredients and delicious enough that I can be proud to serve it.

GREEN CURRY PASTE
(or 2 to 4 tablespoons [22 to 44 g] store-bought)

1 tablespoon (6 g) coriander

1½ teaspoons cumin

10 Thai green chiles

5 serrano chiles

5 stalks lemongrass

3 kaffir lime leaves

1 ounce (28 g) grated ginger

7 cloves garlic

1 bunch cilantro, roots intact

3 stalks basil, stalks intact

1 bunch scallions

2 tablespoons (30 ml) fish sauce

Vegetable oil, as needed

BEEF FILLING

½ head cauliflower

15 baby corn

1½ pounds (680 g) sirloin

1 tablespoon vegetable oil

4 ounces (112 g) crumbled queso blanco cheese

MAKE THE PASTE: Clean and rinse all the ingredients for the curry paste and blend them in the food processor with a little vegetable oil until smooth.

MAKE THE FILLING: Chop the cauliflower into bite-size pieces. Chop the baby corn in half or thirds. Slice the sirloin against the grain into thin slices. Get a little vegetable oil into a hot pan and toss in the meat. After searing it for 1 minute, add in the rest of the veggies and about 2 tablespoons (30 g) of the curry paste. Cook for another 2 minutes, stirring, and then remove from the heat. Stir in the cheese and set aside.

(continued)

Green Curry Beef Enchiladas (cont.)

COCONUT CURRY SAUCE

1 tablespoon vegetable oil

2 (14-ounce [392-g]) cans coconut milk

20 small corn tortillas

4 ounces (112 g) crumbled queso blanco cheese

MAKE THE SAUCE: Clean the pan and get some oil going again. Add in the rest of the curry paste and cook for about 2 minutes, stirring the whole time. Add in your coconut milk and stir well to combine everything. Let it simmer for about 10 minutes.

STUFF IT!: Brush some of the curry sauce onto the bottom of a baking pan. Dip a tortilla into the curry sauce. Add a few tablespoons of the meat mixture to the tortilla. Gently roll up the enchilada. Put the enchilada into the baking dish, seam side down, and brush more of the sauce onto the tortilla. Repeat with the rest of your tortillas. Your pan should be nicely packed with enchiladas. Top with any excess sauce, followed by the cheese.

COOK IT: Preheat the oven to 375°F (190°C, or gas mark 5). Bake the enchiladas for 30 minutes, until the cheese is nicely browned and the tamale mixture is cooked through.

Bulgogi Calzones

MAKES: 2 HUGE CALZONES
HEAT: 3
PIG-OUT SCALE: 6.6

Bulgogi meat has been used as a cheesesteak replacement for years in the colleges and ethnic suburbs of Philly, so I thought that it was only logical to stuff it into a calzone. These calzones came out insanely flavorful and savory, and in my opinion, beat cheesesteak calzones any day of the week.

MARINADE

2 cloves garlic

1-inch (2.5-cm) piece ginger

2 teaspoons chile flakes

1½ teaspoons brown sugar

1½ tablespoons (12 g) gochujang

2 tablespoons (30 ml) rice wine vinegar

3 tablespoons (45 ml) soy sauce

3 tablespoons (45 ml) sesame oil

BEEF FILLING

1 pound (454 g) shaved beef

1 green pepper

1 medium onion

2 carrots

Butter or oil, for sautéing

DIPPING SAUCE

1½ cups (368 g) kimchi

1 batch homemade Pizza Dough (page 194) or 2 packages refrigerated or frozen pizza dough

10 slices American cheese

MAKE THE MARINADE: Make a paste from the garlic and ginger using a microplane or food processor. Mix the garlic, ginger, chile flakes, brown sugar, gochujang, rice wine vinegar, soy sauce and sesame oil to make the bulgogi marinade.

MAKE THE FILLING: Add the shaved beef to the marinade and let it sit for an hour. Thinly slice the pepper, onion and carrots. Add the beef with all the marinade to a hot pan and simmer over medium heat for about 15 minutes until cooked through and sauce has thickened. Brown the veggies in a separate pan with some butter or oil.

MAKE THE DIPPING SAUCE: Take the kimchi and put it into the food processor. Blend to form a smooth sauce. if the sauce seems too thick, add a splash of vinegar to thin it out a bit.

STUFF IT!: Roll out the pizza dough (if using homemade, cut in half for 2 calzones) and start building your calzones starting with cheese, then the veggies and meat mixed together. Top with some more cheese. Fold the dough over the meats and seal the calzone. Place onto a baking sheet. Pierce the top of the dough a few times with a fork to allow the steam to escape. Repeat with second dough.

COOK IT: Preheat the oven to 400˚F (200˚C, or gas mark 6). Bake the calzones for about 25 minutes, until the dough is fully cooked.

vii. Rice paper

vi. Crispy bacon

i. Hard boiled egg

ii. Juicy tomato

v. Crumbled Blue Chee

iii. Shredded lettuce

iv. Ripe avacado

CHAPTER 2:

Stuffed Pasta and Rice

I know I can be goofy or irreverent most of the time, but let me be clear about one thing here. Stuffed pasta is the most important thing that has happened in the history of all things. Sitting in a kitchen with some flour, eggs and a pasta roller has strengthened not only my cooking ability but also the bond I share with my family and loved ones.

Turns out that if you make stuffed pasta for someone, they will love it. If you make stuffed pasta WITH someone, they will think it's the best thing he or she has ever eaten. It's creating memories while creating little packaged morsels of deliciousness.

In this chapter, we go to Asia for some wontons, Europe for pierogi and of course Italy for ravioli. Then things start getting weird when Indian food goes into pasta, lobster is wrapped in mac and cheese and deep-fried and we put a whole burger into a ravioli and stick the thing on a bun. Get ready!

Vietnamese Summer Rolls

Where I grew up there is a huge Vietnamese community, but it still took me a while to start liking their food. When I fell though, I fell hard. Now I am totally addicted to the flavors! These summer rolls are a super easy appetizer to pull together and your friends will be pretty impressed by your mastery of exotic techniques. Just make sure you have extra rice paper around if you have never done it before because it takes a few to really get the hang of wrapping these nice and tight.

MAKES: 8 LARGE SUMMER ROLLS
HEAT: 2.5
PIG-OUT SCALE: 1

DIPPING SAUCE

½ cup (120 ml) hoisin

1 tablespoon (15 ml) mirin

1 tablespoon (15 ml) Sriracha

2 tablespoons (16 g) crushed peanuts

ROLLS

8 rice paper wrappers

24 mint leaves

4 ounces (112 g) rice vermicelli noodles

1 cup (70 g) shredded lettuce

½ cup (65 g) shredded carrot

½ cup (60 g) shredded cucumber

16 cooked medium shrimp

MAKE THE DIPPING SAUCE: Mix the hoisin, mirin and Sriracha in a small bowl. Top with the crushed peanuts. Set aside.

STUFF IT!: Prep all the ingredients and place them around a clean surface for rolling. Fill a shallow bowl with warm water. Dip your rice paper into the water as quick as you can. Just get it in there and take it out, only leaving it in the water for about a second. It will still feel too firm, but the water will continue to soak in and the final texture will be just right. Place the wrapper on the rolling surface and start putting the ingredients on. Start by laying 3 mint leaves flat on the wrapper. Next add the noodles and lettuce, then add the carrot and cucumber. Top with 2 pieces of shrimp. Wrap the paper into a nice tight roll. Repeat with the rest of the rolls. Slice the rolls in half so that each half roll has one piece of shrimp. Serve with the dipping sauce.

You might be surprised just how readily available rice papers are. I find them at almost any grocery store in the Asian section, usually hidden away on the bottom shelf.

Caprese Summer Rolls

MAKES: 8 LARGE SUMMER ROLLS
HEAT: 0
PIG-OUT SCALE: 2.3

ROLLS

Salt

16 tomato slices (about 3 tomatoes)

8 rice paper wrappers

24 basil leaves

16 salami slices

16 slices fresh mozzarella (about 3 large mozzarella balls)

Balsamic vinaigrette, for dipping

This recipe is Vietalian food at its best. My sister and I are both obsessed with Italian and Vietnamese foods, so I am constantly trying to figure out how to blend the two. This recipe uses the summer roll technique to wrap some tasty caprese ingredients for a light snack that is sure to please any palate.

• •

STUFF IT!: Prep all the ingredients and get them ready to roll. Lightly salt the tomato slices. Place them all around a clean surface for rolling. Fill a shallow bowl with warm water. Dip your rice paper into the water as quick as you can. Just get it in there and take it out, only leaving it in the water for about a second. It will still feel too firm, but the water will continue to soak in and the final texture will be just right. Place the wrapper on the rolling surface and start putting the ingredients in. Start by laying 3 basil leaves flat on the wrapper. Next add 2 slices of salami, then add 2 slices each of the tomato and cheese. Wrap the paper into a nice tight roll. Repeat with the rest of the rolls. Slice the rolls in half, and serve with the balsamic vinaigrette for dipping.

Cobb Summer Rolls

MAKES: 4 LARGE SUMMER ROLLS
HEAT: 0
PIG-OUT SCALE: 3.9

Vietnamese summer rolls are really just a salad in a wrapper, so I expanded this idea by putting a different salad into this same wrapper. The bacon is really what makes this Cobb summer roll work, but when assembled right and each bite has all of the components it's a perfect way to eat the salad.

. . . .

ROLLS

1 avocado

2 vine-ripened tomatoes

1 hard-boiled egg

Salt

2 slices bacon

4 rice paper wrappers

1 cup (70 g) shredded lettuce

Blue cheese dressing, for dipping

MAKE THE ROLLS: Slice the avocado, tomatoes and egg and lightly salt. Cook the bacon in a skillet over medium heat until the fat is rendered and the bacon is crispy. Cut each slice in half or crumble into a bowl. Place all of the ingredients around a clean surface for rolling. Fill a shallow bowl with warm water. Dip your rice paper into the water as quick as you can. Just get it in there and take it out, only leaving it in the water for about a second. It will still feel too firm, but the water will continue to soak in and the final texture will be just right. Place the wrapper on the rolling surface and start putting the ingredients in. Start by placing the lettuce on the wrapper. Next add the tomatoes, then add the egg and avocado. Top with the bacon. Wrap the paper into a nice tight summer roll. Repeat with the rest of the rolls. Serve with the blue cheese dressing.

Loaded Potato Pierogi

MAKES: 24 PIEROGI
HEAT: 3.7
PIG-OUT SCALE: 9.5

DOUGH

2 cups (240 g) flour, plus more for dusting

1 egg

¼ cup (60 ml) milk

½ cup (112 g) sour cream

½ teaspoon salt

FILLING

3 large potatoes

Salt

1 onion

4 tablespoons (56 g) butter

8 ounces (225 g) Cheddar cheese

Pierogi is a Polish take on a ravioli or pot sticker that is commonly filled with potato, onion and cheese. My favorite thing about them though is the use of sour cream in the pasta dough. It adds a really subtle tang to the mix and separates these from all the other ethnic varieties.

This recipe treats the pierogi like a baked potato, making a sauce out of the butter and sour cream, and loading on the rest of the ingredients. If you prefer broccoli, baked beans, nacho cheese or anything else on your baked potato, go ahead and use those instead.

• •

MAKE THE DOUGH: Mix the dough ingredients together in a bowl. It should be a thick dough that is easy to knead. Add more flour if needed. Pour out onto a work surface and knead for about 5 to 7 minutes just to smooth it out a bit. Place the dough in the fridge for a half hour to rest.

MAKE THE FILLING: Peel and chop the potatoes into rough 2-inch (5-cm) chunks. Place into a pot of cold salted water and bring to a simmer. Cook until tender, about 30 minutes, then strain the potatoes. Meanwhile, dice the onion. Melt the butter in a frying pan and sauté the onion until softened, about 5 minutes. Add salt to taste. Pour the butter and onion mixture over the potatoes and mash until smooth. Stir in the cheese. Taste and add salt if needed.

STUFF IT!: Roll out your dough to about ⅛ inch (3 mm) thick. This is traditionally done with a rolling pin instead of a pasta roller. Cut out about 3-inch (7.5-cm) rounds using a cookie cutter or the top of a glass. Fill your dough with the potato filling and fold over into a half-moon shape. Seal by wetting your finger and brushing it along the edge of the dough. Use a fork to make decorative lines along the edge and also further seal the pierogi.

(continued)

VERY BASIC CHILI

2 large onions

1 bell pepper

5 cloves garlic

2 habanero peppers

1 pound (454 g) ground beef

1 tablespoon (15 ml) olive oil

Salt

1 tablespoon (6 g) chili powder

1 teaspoon cumin

1 (28-ounce [784 g]) can diced tomatoes

1 teaspoon oregano

TOPPINGS AND SAUCE

8 slices bacon

4 tablespoons (56 g) butter

1 clove garlic

1 cup (225 g) sour cream

Splash of milk

Handful of chives

Shredded Cheddar cheese

MAKE THE CHILI: Dice the onions and bell pepper. Mince the garlic and habanero. In a skillet over medium heat, brown the ground beef in a little bit of olive oil. Season with salt. Once fully cooked, remove from the pan. Drain most of the fat but leave about 1 tablespoon (15 ml) to start the veggies in. Sauté the onions and bell pepper in the fat with salt. After about 10 minutes, when the onions are just starting to brown, stir in the habanero and garlic. Cook for 1 minute, then add the chili powder and cumin. Stir and mix nonstop for 1 minute before adding the can of tomatoes and the oregano. Mix well and let simmer for at least 30 minutes. If it seems dry, simmer with the cover on; if it seems wet, simmer with the cover off.

PREP THE TOPPINGS AND MAKE THE SAUCE: Dice the bacon and cook it slow and low to render out the fat and crisp it up nicely, about 10 minutes. Remove from the pan and drain the fat, leaving just enough to barely coat the pan. Toss in the butter and garlic and simmer while the butter melts, about 1 minute. Remove from the heat. Add the sour cream and mix well to create the sauce. Mix in a splash of milk just to loosen it.

COOK IT: Bring a large pot of water to a boil, add the pierogi, and cook for about 5 to 7 minutes, until they are floating and the pasta is tender. Toss the pierogi in the sauce to coat them all nicely. Serve on a plate topped with the chili, crisp bacon, chives and cheese.

Truffled Caramelized Onion and Ricotta Pierogi

MAKES: 24 PIEROGI
HEAT: 0
PIG-OUT SCALE: 6.0

1 batch Dough (page 61)

FILLING
1 large potato
Salt
1 large onion
1 tablespoon (14 g) butter
1 tablespoon (15 ml) or more truffle oil
4 ounces (112 g) ricotta cheese

Take your pierogi to the next level. A few slight tweaks to the recipe turn this peasant dish into something elegant. Make these mini and you could serve them as an app at a black tie event!

• •

MAKE THE DOUGH: Make the dough following the recipe for Loaded Potato Pierogi (page 61).

MAKE THE FILLING: Peel and chop the potato into rough 2-inch (5-cm) chunks. Place into a pot of cold salted water and bring to a simmer. Cook until tender, about 30 minutes, then strain the potatoes. Meanwhile, dice the onion. Melt the butter in a frying pan and sauté the onion low and slow until deeply browned, about 20 minutes. Add salt to taste. Add the onions and truffle oil to the potatoes and mash until smooth. Stir in the cheese. Taste and salt if needed.

STUFF AND COOK: Stuff the pierogi and cook following the directions on pages 61 to 62.

Aloo Gobi Pierogi

MAKES: 24 PIEROGI
HEAT: 2.1
PIG-OUT SCALE: 6.0

1 batch Dough (page 61)

FILLING
2 large potatoes
Salt
½ onion
¼ large head cauliflower
2 tablespoons (28 g) butter
1½ teaspoons curry powder, homemade (page 191) or store-bought
1 (14-ounce [392-g]) can diced tomatoes
½ cup (65 g) peas

This recipe is the result of a samosa and pierogi love affair. The flavors just work so well that the recipe practically wrote itself. Serve these with a little clarified butter for dipping.

• •

MAKE THE DOUGH: Make the dough following the recipe for Loaded Potato Pierogi (page 61).

MAKE THE FILLING: Peel and chop the potatoes into rough 2-inch (5-cm) chunks. Place into a pot of cold salted water and bring to a simmer. Cook until tender, about 30 minutes, then strain the potatoes. Meanwhile, dice the onion and the cauliflower. Melt the butter in a frying pan and sauté the onion until softened, about 5 minutes. Add salt to taste. Add the cauliflower and sauté, stirring well, for another 5 minutes. Add the curry powder. Add the tomatoes to the pan along with the peas. Bring to a simmer and cook for about 15 minutes, then remove from the heat. Pour the cauliflower mixture over the potatoes and mash until it is a nice chunky mixture with fairly smooth potatoes. Taste and add salt if needed.

STUFF AND COOK: Stuff the pierogi and cook following the directions on pages 61 to 62.

Tamale Ravioli

MAKES: 6 TO 8 RAVIOLI
HEAT: 8.6
PIG-OUT SCALE: 3.9

1 batch Fresh Pasta Dough (page 193)

SAUCE
½ pound (225 g) ground beef

1 onion, diced

3 cloves garlic, minced

1 can chipotle in adobo

1 (28-ounce [784-g]) can crushed tomatoes

1 cup (235 ml) cream

FILLING
1 cup (120 g) masa harina

1 cup (130 g) corn, fresh or frozen

1 jalapeño, diced and seeded

¼ cup (16 g) chopped cilantro

8 ounces (225 g) grated cheese

Salt

1½ cups (355 ml) water, or as needed

Just when you guys thought we were done with the tamales from the last chapter, here we are with some more! But don't worry, this recipe is unique and fun and totally deserves its spot here. The key is to really stuff the tamale filling into these ravs so that when you take a bite the spicy chipotle sauce is counteracted by the fluffy, cooling corn filling.

• •

MAKE THE PASTA DOUGH: Prepare the Fresh Pasta Dough recipe from page 193 and set aside in the refrigerator.

MAKE THE SAUCE: In a skillet over medium heat, brown the ground beef, remove from the pan, then drain most of the fat but keep some in the pan. Sauté the onion in the remaining fat until it starts to brown, about 5 minutes. Add the garlic and cook for 2 minutes. Meanwhile, open the can of chipotle peppers and pour it out onto your cutting board. Try your best to remove a lot of the seeds from the peppers in the can if you don't want this sauce to be insanely hot. Dice up the peppers and add them to the pan along with the liquid from the can. Cook for a few more minutes, then add the tomatoes. Add the beef back in along with ¾ cup (180 ml) of the cream and let this simmer slowly for about an hour. Finish with the remaining ¼ cup (60 ml) cream just before serving.

MAKE THE FILLING: Combine the masa harina, corn, jalapeño, cilantro, cheese and salt to taste in a bowl. Slowly add the water and stir until it becomes a thick pasty texture similar to that of peanut butter.

STUFF IT!: Put out a small cup of water to dip your fingers and help seal the pasta later. Divide your pasta dough into 3 balls. Roll out your pasta, kneading it by rolling it on the thickest setting on the pasta maker, folding it over on itself, and repeating 3 to 5 times. Cut each sheet in half and roll them out to the second thinnest setting on your pasta maker. Put one of the pasta sheets on your work surface. Every 3 inches (7.5 cm), put a heaping tablespoon of the tamale mixture in the center of the pasta sheet. Lightly wet the area of the pasta dough around the filling using your finger. Put another sheet of pasta dough on top and work around the filling of each ravioli to remove as much air as possible and seal everything up nicely. Use a ravioli cutter (or pizza cutter) to form ravioli squares. Lay out an old tablecloth or bed sheet and lightly flour it. Allow your ravioli to dry on the sheet as you roll out more. Be sure to re-roll the scrap pieces to form as many ravioli as possible from the dough.

COOK IT: Boil the pasta in a few batches so as not to crowd the water. When the pasta is floating and fully cooked, about 5 minutes, put it right into the sauce and gently mix. Serve.

Soft Yolk Ravioli

This is a fun and unique type of ravioli where the egg yolk only slightly cooks and as you cut into the ravioli a new sauce is formed, giving the pasta a flavor profile similar to carbonara. Don't expect to make this for a large group, though, because this dish is best for a more intimate couple setting, with each person getting 3 large ravioli.

MAKES: 6 LARGE RAVIOLI
HEAT: 1.4
PIG-OUT SCALE: 5

• •

½ batch Fresh Pasta Dough (page 193)

SAUCE

6 strips bacon

1 tablespoon (15 ml) olive oil

2 cloves garlic, minced

½ cup (120 ml) light cream

1 ¼ cup (285 g) ricotta cheese

¼ cup (16 g) chopped parsley

¼ cup (45 g) Parmesan cheese, for serving

Salt and pepper, to taste

Additional Parm and black pepper, for serving

6 egg yolks

MAKE THE PASTA DOUGH: Prepare half of the Fresh Pasta Dough recipe from page 193 and set aside in the refrigerator.

MAKE THE SAUCE: Chop the bacon into smaller strips. In a skillet, cook the bacon in some olive oil over medium heat until the fat has rendered and the bacon is just about crispy. Remove about half of the fat. Toss in the garlic and cook for 1 minute. Add in the cream and bring to a simmer before removing from the heat.

STUFF IT!: Mix the ricotta with the parm and parsley. Season with salt and pepper. Roll out the pasta dough and stuff following the directions on page 65, first putting some ricotta down, almost as a cradle for the egg yolk. Drop the yolk into the ricotta cradle and gently seal and form the ravioli.

COOK IT: Boil the pasta in a few batches so as not to crowd the water. When the pasta is floating and fully cooked, about 3 minutes, put it right into the sauce and gently mix. Top with the Parm, parsley mixture and black pepper, and serve.

Chicken Tikka Masala Ravioli

MAKES: 24 RAVIOLI
HEAT: 2.5
PIG-OUT SCALE: 5.1

I consider this recipe to be my signature dish. Each bite sums up exactly the way I cook. Classic styles presented in new ways. Dishes that everyone knows, mixed with a hint of the exotic. Not only do these ravioli exemplify my cooking style, but they are also one of the most delicious things I have ever made. It was a revelation to me to add grilled ingredients inside ravioli. When you take a bite of this dish, what looks like a normal ravioli gives way to surprise after surprise of Indian spices and smoky grilled flavor.

· ·

1 batch Fresh Pasta Dough (page 193)

FILLING

2 cups (450 g) yogurt
1 tablespoon (6 g) cumin
1 tablespoon (6 g) curry powder
2 teaspoons smoked paprika
2 pounds (908 g) chicken thighs
2 red onions
Melted butter, for brushing the onions
1 cup (150 g) crumbled paneer cheese

SAUCE

2 Thai chiles
1-inch (2.5-cm) piece ginger
3 cloves garlic
1 tablespoon (6 g) curry powder
1 tablespoon (14 g) butter
1 (28-ounce [784-g]) can crushed tomatoes
½ cup (120 ml) cream

Chopped cilantro, for garnish

MAKE THE PASTA DOUGH: Prepare the Fresh Pasta Dough recipe from page 193 and set aside in the refrigerator.

MAKE THE FILLING: Combine the yogurt, cumin, curry powder and smoked paprika in a small bowl. The yogurt should turn a nice shade of pink. Taste to make sure it is seasoned to your liking, and then add the chicken, turning to coat in the sauce. Cover with plastic and allow this to sit in the fridge overnight.

The next day, slice the onions and brush with melted butter. Grill the chicken and onions over a medium-high flame until everything is cooked and has a nice char on it, approximately 25 minutes. Dice up the cooked chicken and onions and mix in a large bowl with the paneer cheese.

STUFF IT!: Roll out the pasta dough and stuff following the directions on page 65.

MAKE THE SAUCE: Blend the chiles, ginger, garlic and curry powder into a paste in a food processor. Melt the butter in a skillet over medium heat, add the paste and sauté for 1 minute. Add the tomatoes and cream, and simmer for 10 minutes.

COOK IT: Boil the ravioli for about 6 minutes, gently stirring occasionally. When the pasta is cooked, add it right to the warm sauce and stir to combine. Sprinkle with the cilantro and serve immediately.

Almost everything in this recipe can be made ahead. If you make the ravioli early, it is a good idea to freeze them on a baking sheet, then put them into a zip-top bag when they are frozen.

Mac and Cheese Ravioli

Once I came up with a mac and cheese recipe that solidified when it was cooled down, I knew the possibilities were endless. One of the first examples of me playing around with this idea is in these mac and cheese stuffed raviolis. This dish represents my favorite foods inside one another: a perfect tomato sauce and tender homemade pasta, wrapped around creamy mac and cheese. If this incorporated pizza somehow I think my head would explode.

1 batch Fresh Pasta Dough (page 193)

MAC AND CHEESE

8 ounces (225 g) pasta

½ small onion, diced

1½ tablespoons (21 g) butter

1 clove garlic, minced

1½ tablespoons (12 g) flour

1½ cups (355 ml) milk

8 ounces (225 g) Cheddar cheese, grated

8 ounces (225 g) Monterey Jack cheese, grated

Salt

1 recipe Simple Marinara sauce (page 194)

MAKE THE PASTA DOUGH: Prepare the Fresh Pasta Dough recipe from page 193 and set aside in the refrigerator.

MAKE THE MAC AND CHEESE: Bring water to a boil in a medium pot and cook your pasta according to package directions, until al dente. Meanwhile, in a skillet over medium heat, cook the onion in the butter for about 5 minutes. Toss in the garlic. Next add the flour and whisk well to combine. Cook for about 3 minutes, stirring the whole time, until the flour turns a slightly toasted hue. Add the milk and whisk well to eliminate any lumps. Bring to a simmer and remove from the heat. Add the pasta, then mix in the cheeses. Stir until all the cheese melts, which should happen naturally, but you can put it back onto low heat if necessary. Taste and add salt if necessary. Pour the pasta into a 9 x 13-inch (23 x 33 cm) pan and smooth out to a thin layer. Refrigerate until hardened, about 2 hours. Cut into 1½-inch (3.8 cm) squares.

STUFF IT!: Roll out the pasta dough and stuff following the directions on page 65.

COOK IT: Boil the pasta in a few batches so as not to crowd the water. When the pasta is floating and fully cooked, about 5 minutes, put it right into the sauce and gently mix. Serve.

Fish Ravioli in Thai Red Curry

MAKES: 24 RAVIOLI
HEAT: 6.3
PIG-OUT SCALE: 3.1

You may have already noticed that I like to play around with Thai curry pastes. To me, they are almost like a pesto and can be used as such in a variety of dishes. The juxtaposition of the two familiar flavors in this dish creates something entirely new on the palate. A little bit of work? Maybe, but you could really impress people with this one. The filling works with cod, haddock or halibut.

• •

1 batch Fresh Pasta Dough (page 193)

CURRY PASTE
(or 2 to 4 tablespoons [22 to 44 g] store-bought)

15 dried red chiles

3 cardamom pods or a pinch of cardamom powder

3 tablespoons (18 g) chopped lemongrass

2-inch (5 cm) piece ginger

7 cloves garlic

3 shallots

2 tablespoons (30 ml) fish sauce

1 teaspoon salt

1 tablespoon (6 g) cumin

1 tablespoon (6 g) coriander

1 clove

¼ teaspoon cinnamon

2 to 4 tablespoons (30 to 60 ml) vegetable oil

FILLING

¾ pound (340 g) mild white fish

Salt

24 whole cilantro leaves

SAUCE

1 green bell pepper

20 baby corn

1 tablespoon (15 ml) vegetable oil

2 cans coconut milk

1 teaspoon brown sugar

½ pound (225 g) squid

2 cups (120 g) torn Thai basil

MAKE THE PASTA DOUGH: Prepare the Fresh Pasta Dough recipe from page 193 and set aside in the refrigerator.

MAKE THE CURRY PASTE: Depending on how hot you want it, you can take out some or all of the seeds from the chile peppers. Grind the chiles in a spice grinder along with the cardamom if you are using whole spices. Put all the ingredients including the spice mix into a food processor and purée, adding more vegetable oil if needed

MAKE THE FILLING: Chop the fish into about 1-inch (2.5-cm) chunks and season lightly with salt.

MAKE THE SAUCE: Chop up the pepper and corn into bite-size pieces. In a hot pan with a little vegetable oil, fry the curry paste for about 2 minutes, stirring constantly. Stir the coconut milk, brown sugar, pepper and corn. Simmer for 15 minutes.

STUFF IT!: Roll out the pasta dough and stuff following the directions on page 65, putting a piece of fish and a single cilantro leaf in center of each ravioli.

COOK IT: Then, clean and chop the squid into rings and tentacles. Drop the ravioli into a pot of boiling water. You may need to do this in 2 batches so as not to crowd the pot. Right after you drop the ravioli into the water, add the squid and basil to the simmering curry sauce. Cook for about 1½ minutes and remove from the heat. Strain the ravioli into the sauce and stir well but gently. Serve.

Teriyaki Ravioli

MAKES: 24 RAVIOLI
HEAT: 1.3
PIG-OUT SCALE: 6.2

1 batch Fresh Pasta Dough (page 193)

SAUCE
1 recipe Cream Sauce (page 195)
1 cup (30 g) chopped spinach

FILLING
2 tablespoons (12 g) grated ginger
2 tablespoons (20 g) grated garlic
2 tablespoons (16 g) sesame seeds
1 tablespoon (15 ml) Sriracha
¼ cup (60 g) brown sugar
2 tablespoons (30 ml) rice vinegar
Black pepper
1 cup (235 ml) soy sauce, or as needed
1½ pounds (680 g) chicken tenders

The first time I tried the teriyaki-Alfredo combo was at a place called Michael's Pasta in the Pan in Agawam, Massachusetts. My friend Steph had previously sung its praises to me but I was skeptical. When I finally tried it I was mesmerized by the way the sharp salty teriyaki really cuts through the creamy Alfredo. I knew I would have to make it at home some way or another! Instead of chicken teriyaki resting on a bed of creamy fettuccine Alfredo, I decided to keep the teriyaki flavor trapped in ravioli. This way, it's almost a surprise as you bite into your first one and the teriyaki flavor comes exploding out.

• •

MAKE THE PASTA DOUGH: Prepare the Fresh Pasta Sauce dough recipe from page 193 and set aside in the refrigerator.

MAKE THE SAUCE: Prepare the cream sauce and add the chopped spinach.

MAKE THE FILLING: In a large bowl, combine the ginger, garlic, sesame seeds, Sriracha, brown sugar, vinegar, pepper to taste and soy sauce. Add the chicken and turn to coat. Cover with plastic wrap and allow to marinate for a few hours in the refrigerator.

Remove the chicken from the marinade, reserving the marinade. Place the chicken on a baking sheet and broil for about 5 minutes per side until lightly browned and cooked through. Meanwhile, bring the reserved marinade to a rapid boil and boil for at least 10 minutes to kill any raw chicken bacteria. Lightly simmer this until it is reduced into a syrup. Shred the chicken in a large bowl and taste for seasoning. Add some of your teriyaki syrup if it needs more flavor. The teriyaki flavor needs to be really strong so it cuts through the pasta and cream sauce, but you also don't want the mixture too wet or it will seep through the pasta while it is resting. I usually use about half of the syrup.

STUFF IT!: Roll out the pasta dough and stuff following the directions on page 65.

COOK IT: Boil the pasta in a few batches so as not to crowd the water. When the pasta is floating and fully cooked, about 5 minutes, put it right into the sauce and gently mix. Serve.

Manicotti

MAKES: 6 SERVINGS
HEAT: 0
PIG-OUT SCALE: 5.2

Manicotti was always my favorite food growing up, and it was the meal my mom would cook for me on my birthday. It is a true example of the magic that happens when simple ingredients are put together in such a way that makes them more than what they are. I like to make this dish with homemade ricotta to really drive the "from scratch" element home. If you haven't made ricotta at home, put down the book and make this dish tonight.

RICOTTA

1 gallon (3.8 L) milk
1 quart (940 ml) buttermilk

1 recipe Fresh Pasta Dough (page 193)

FILLING

¼ cup (16 g) chopped parsley
½ cup (50 g) grated Parmesan
1 egg
Salt and pepper

1 recipe Meaty Tomato Sauce (page 193) or Simple Marinara (page 194)
1 cup (150 g) grated mozzarella
2 teaspoons salt

MAKE THE RICOTTA: Mix the milk and buttermilk in a large, heavy-bottomed pot with a thermometer. Heat on medium-high heat, scraping the bottom often with a wooden or heatproof rubber spatula. Bring to 165°F (74°C) (you will see the curds separate from the whey at this point.) Remove from the heat, tossing in a few ice cubes just to make sure it doesn't overheat. Let it sit for another 10 minutes or so, and pour into a colander lined with cheesecloth. Place the colander in a large bowl. Lightly cover and let it sit in the fridge draining for about an hour while you make your pasta and prep the rest of the ingredients.

MAKE THE PASTA: Roll out your pasta to the thinnest setting and cut it into large squares. Basically, leave the width the same and cut it the long way to make the pieces square. Bring a pot of salted water to a boil, add the pasta and boil for 2 to 3 minutes, or until cooked.

MAKE THE FILLING: Combine the homemade ricotta with the parsley, Parmesan and egg, and season with salt and pepper if needed.

STUFF IT!: Once all the pasta is all cooked, prepare your work surface for filling. On each square of pasta, put a nice ¼ cup (60 g) of the ricotta mixture and roll it up into a cigar shape. The pasta should overlap for about half of the circumference of the circle. Lightly sauce the bottom of the baking dish you will be using, and line up the manicotti in the dish, seam side down. Add more sauce to the top, followed by the mozzarella.

COOK IT: Preheat the oven to 450°F (230°C, or gas mark 8). Bake until just heated through, about 30 minutes, then turn on the broiler and broil for a minute to brown the cheese on top.

Carnitas Burrito Manicotti

MAKES: 6 SERVINGS

HEAT: 6.1

PIG-OUT SCALE: 7.7

I work in a burrito shop where I created all of the recipes we use. I feel like I had been researching for that role my whole life! During the recipe testing phases for the burrito place, I would often come home with extra ingredients, and that's where this recipe idea came from. Why not wrap the burrito in pasta instead of a tortilla?

SAUCE

3 tablespoons (42 g) butter

½ onion, diced

3 tablespoons (24 g) flour

3 cups (705 ml) milk

6 ounces (168 g) Cheddar cheese, grated

12 ounces (340 g) Monterey Jack cheese, grated

1 (16-ounce [450-g]) can diced tomatoes with green chiles

1 recipe Fresh Pasta Dough (page 193)

1 cup (165 g) cooked rice

1 (15-ounce [420-g]) can black beans, drained and rinsed

About 2 cups (400 g) Carnitas (page 190)

Pico de Gallo, homemade (page 190) or store-bought

Chipotle hot sauce

MAKE THE SAUCE: Heat the butter over medium heat in a Dutch oven or heavy-bottomed pot. Add the onion and let it sweat for about 7 to 8 minutes. Add the flour and stir well, cooking for about 3 to 5 minutes. Whisk in the milk, being sure to get any lumps out, and bring to a simmer. Once the sauce reaches a simmer, remove from the heat. Drop in the cheeses and whisk until melted. Finally, strain the can of tomatoes and stir it in.

STUFF IT!: Roll out your pasta to the thinnest setting and cut it into large squares. Basically, leave the width the same and cut it the long way to make the pieces square. Bring a pot of water to a boil and boil the pasta squares for about 2 to 3 minutes, until cooked. Meanwhile, line up all of your ingredients for assembly.

On each square of pasta, add about a tablespoon each of rice, beans, carnitas and pico de gallo. Add a dab of hot sauce and roll it up into a cigar shape. The pasta should overlap for about half of the circumference of the circle. Lightly sauce the bottom of the baking dish you will be using, and line up the manicotti in the dish, seam side down. Add more sauce to the top.

COOK IT: Preheat the oven to 450°F (230°C, or gas mark 8). Bake until bubbly and browned on top.

Couscous Salad Stuffed Shells

MAKES: 6 SERVINGS
HEAT: 2.2
PIG-OUT SCALE: 4.2

I've been making this couscous pasta salad for years, but it was only after I began putting it into shells that people started asking for the recipe. I didn't change a thing about the salad itself, but the presentation caused people to really be impressed by it! I think what's great about serving it this way is that people at a cookout can just grab their pre-portioned amount and dig in. You can even eat it with your hands if you forgot to grab a fork!

1 pound (454 g) jumbo pasta shells

FILLING

2 cups (350 g) couscous

1 bunch scallions

1 bunch basil

6 vine-ripened tomatoes

8 ounces (225 g) cojita cheese (use ricotta salata or even feta if you can't find it)

1 clove garlic

2 tablespoons (22 g) Dijon mustard

¼ cup (60 ml) red wine vinegar, plus more for drizzling

1 tablespoon (4 g) red pepper flakes

¼ cup (60 ml) olive oil, plus more for drizzling

½ teaspoon salt

½ teaspoon pepper

MAKE THE PASTA: Bring salted pasta water in a pot to a boil. Add the shells and cook according to package directions until al dente, then remove from the pot.

MAKE THE FILLING: Cook the couscous in boiling water according to package directions until tender, and then strain in a mesh strainer. Meanwhile, chop up the scallions and basil and dice the tomatoes. Crumble the cheese. Grate the garlic with a mesh grater. Mix the cooked couscous with all of the ingredients except for the cheese; mix in the cheese once the pasta has cooled a bit.

STUFF IT!: Stuff the couscous filling into the pasta shells and line them up in a dish. Drizzle with a little extra oil and vinegar. Serve as a side at a barbecue.

Saag Paneer Stuffed Shells

MAKES: 6 SERVINGS
HEAT: 1.9
PIG-OUT SCALE: 4.2

Stuffed shell recipes often have a decent amount of spinach in them along with the ricotta cheese. This made me think of the Indian dish saag paneer that also has lots of spinach with bits of cheese in it. Finally, one day I put them together and it was a flavor pairing I will never forget.

• •

MAKE THE FILLING: Cube the cheese into very small (½-inch [1.3-cm]) cubes. Grate the garlic and ginger and mix together with the curry powder to make a paste. Dice the onion. Purée the spinach in a food processor. Get the butter into a large frying pan with a splash of oil. The oil will reduce the smoke point of the butter. Fry the cheese cubes in the butter until they start to brown, about 5 minutes. Add the onion and continue to cook until both the onion and the cheese are nicely browned, about 15 minutes. Add the garlic paste and cook for 1 minute. Finally, add the spinach and remove from the heat. Mix well.

STUFF IT!: Boil the shells until they are mostly but not fully cooked, about 9 minutes. Strain, reserving ½ cup (120 ml) of the pasta cooking liquid. Stuff the shells with the cheese spinach curry mixture. Line the shells in a baking dish. Whisk together the yogurt and the reserved pasta water. Pour this mixture over the shells.

COOK IT: Preheat the oven to 350°F (176°C, or gas mark 4). Bake for about 15 to 20 minutes, until lightly browned on top. Serve.

FILLING

16 ounces (450 g) paneer cheese

5 cloves garlic

2-inch (5-cm) piece ginger

1 tablespoon (6 g) curry powder, homemade (page 191) or store-bought

2 large onions

2 pounds (900 g) raw spinach

4 tablespoons (56 g) butter

Olive oil

1 pound (454 g) extra-large shell pasta

1 cup (225 g) yogurt, room temperature

Thai Shrimp Wontons

MAKES: 24 WONTONS
HEAT: 7.4
PIG-OUT SCALE: 3.3

FILLING

5 cloves garlic

2-inch (5-cm) piece ginger

1 tablespoon (6 g) chopped lemongrass

5 Thai chiles

1 shallot

Fish sauce or soy sauce

Vegetable oil

1 pound (454 g) shrimp

24 wonton wrappers

Unlike when I make pasta, I usually use store-bought wonton wrappers when I make any of these varieties. If you are lucky enough to have an Asian grocery store where you live, you can usually find all of the different varieties of dough wrappers. If you really want to delve into making your own dough, there are tons of great recipes online.

• •

MAKE THE FILLING: In a food processor, make a very fine paste from the garlic, ginger, lemongrass, chiles, shallot and some fish or soy sauce. Use a little bit of vegetable oil to help it become a nice fine paste. Cut up the raw shrimp into a small dice and mix with the paste to form the filling.

STUFF IT!: For these wontons, I like to put the filling into the center of the wrapper, and fold all of the sides straight up almost like a cup so you can still see the filling from the top.

COOK IT: Steam the wontons until the filling is cooked through, about 8 minutes. Serve with Thai Sweet and Sour Sauce (page 195) for dipping.

Tortellini Soup

Tortellini soup has been a Christmas Eve tradition in my family for as long as I can remember. This is the exact recipe from my grandmother, cut into a fourth. We normally work with about five people to make 1,000 tortellini in four hours, and not only does it feed twenty-five people on Christmas Eve, but we also usually have about 400 frozen left over to save for a cold day or hand out to relatives. This recipe should make about 250. You could use half and freeze the other half.

• •

FILLING

1 large boneless, skinless chicken breast (about ¼ pound [112 g])

1 or 2 pork chops (about ¼ pound [112 g]), deboned

1 egg

5 slices mortadella

¼ cup (25 g) Parmesan, grated

2 tablespoons (16 g) breadcrumbs

1 small pinch nutmeg

¼ teaspoon salt

½ teaspoon pepper

1 recipe Fresh Pasta Dough (page 193)

1 gallon (3.7 L) chicken stock (preferably homemade)

1 pound (450 g) carrots, cleaned and chopped

MAKE THE FILLING: In batches in a food processor, pulse all of the filling ingredients until it becomes a very fine mixture, but not completely puréed. It needs to be really fine because tortellini are very, very small.

STUFF IT!: Roll out the dough to the thinnest setting and cut 2-inch (5-cm) squares out of the dough. Put about ½ teaspoon of filling on each square and fold it into a triangle, sealing it well. Bring the two far ends together straight back to form the traditional tortellini shape.

Allow these to dry on a bed sheet and then put them into the freezer on a baking sheet so that none touch each other. After they are frozen, you can pack them into plastic zip-top bags.

COOK IT: The soup uses half (125) of the tortellini. It is just a nice big pot of homemade chicken stock simmering away with some carrot. Simmer the tortellini right in the broth with the carrots for about 5 minutes and they are ready.

Korean Pork Mandu

MAKES: 30 MANDU
HEAT: 0
PIG-OUT SCALE: 6.8

My parents actually lived in Korea when they were younger and my Dad was in the Army, but this station didn't translate to me eating bulgogi and bipimbop as a kid. I didn't even know what Korean food was until my friend Amy hosted a Korean party a few years back. My first bite into the flavorful world of Korean cuisine was one these little pork mandu she had made for us. From then on, I was hooked.

FILLING

½ pound (225 g) ground pork

8 ounces (225 g) mushrooms, diced small

1 cup (90 g) diced cabbage

½ cup (65 g) shredded carrot

1 bunch scallions, chopped

1 clove garlic, grated

1-inch (2.5 cm) piece ginger, grated

1 egg

1 tablespoon (15 ml) sesame oil

1 teaspoon salt

30 wonton wrappers

Oil, for frying

MAKE THE FILLING: Mix all the filling ingredients together in a large bowl.

STUFF IT!: Mandu are more traditionally a round wrapper and are folded into a half moon but crimped on top. Put about 2 tablespoons (30 g) of the meat mixture into your wrapper and fold it in half. Starting at one end of the round seam, fold a piece of the wrapper onto itself and press hard to seal. Depending on the brand, you can use water or even an egg wash if your wrappers have trouble sealing on their own. Repeat, folding small portions of the seam onto itself all the way around the half circle to form the iconic crimped edge.

COOK IT: Preheat the oil to 350°F (180°C) and fry the mandu in batches until golden and crispy. Drain on paper towels.

Cheeseburger Ravioli Burger

MAKES: 4 RAVIOLI BURGERS
HEAT: 0
PIG-OUT SCALE: 9.3

Making an extra-large ravioli has been on my to-do list for a while, but I had no idea what would be in it. Like many of my greatest ideas, this one came to me in a dream. A beautiful, beautiful dream. I woke up immediately trying to tell anyone who would listen about this amazing burger that I ate in my dream. Well, sometimes dreams do come true, kids. Two of my favorite foods became one on the very next day.

. . . .

SAUCE

1 large onion

1 tablespoon (14 g) butter

Salt

1 (28-ounce [784 g]) can crushed tomatoes

1 tablespoon (15 ml) Worcestershire sauce

1 teaspoon oregano

BURGERS

A little over 1 pound (454 g) 95% lean ground beef

Salt and pepper

½ recipe Fresh Pasta Dough (page 193)

½ cup (112 g) ricotta cheese

8 slices American cheese

4 burger buns

MAKE THE SAUCE: Slice the onion into thin, ¼-inch (6-mm) round slices. Get the butter into a saucepan over medium heat and add the onions with some salt. Cook the onions until they become very browned, about 20 minutes. Add the crushed tomatoes, Worcestershire and oregano. Taste and add salt if needed. Simmer lightly while you make the rest of the meal.

MAKE THE BURGERS: Divide the meat into 4 equal pieces and form them into burger patties. Season with salt and pepper. In a hot frying pan, sear the burgers for about 2 minutes per side to brown. They will still be fairly undercooked in the center.

STUFF IT!: Roll out your pasta to the third-thinnest setting on your pasta roller. This is a little thicker than normal, but is perfect for a ravioli of this size. Cut your dough into squares that are large enough to contain the burger. On one square, put 2 tablespoons (28 g) of ricotta, then put down the burger. Top with 2 American cheese slices. Finally, top with the second square of pasta. Lightly wet the edges of the dough with your fingers to seal the ravioli as tightly as possible. Use a fork to press down on the edges of the pasta to add decoration on the edges but also to form an additional seal around the burger.

COOK IT: Bring a pot of salted water to a light boil over medium-high heat. Gently drop a ravioli into the water. Keep your eye on it and allow it to lightly simmer away for about 8 minutes, until the pasta is cooked and the burger reaches a nice medium doneness. Slide it onto a bun and serve with the sauce

Cheesesteak Pot Sticker

Cheesesteak is surprisingly the perfect filling for these little half fried/half steamed dumplings of deliciousness. Normally pot stickers aren't associated with cheese, but it goes really well in this application. When you take a bite that has crunchy browned wrapper, gooey soft wrapper, savory meaty filling, and some of that creamy cheese, everything is right in the world.

MAKES: 30 POT STICKERS
HEAT: 3.1
PIG-OUT SCALE: 7.5

FILLING

2 or 3 large onions

2 tablespoons (28 g) butter

1 ¼ pounds (568 g) shaved rib eye (but any shaved steak will work)

1 cup (135 g) sliced banana peppers

8 ounces (225 g) Monterey Jack, American or provolone cheese (or a mixture), grated or crumbled

30 wonton wrappers

Oil, for frying

¼ cup (60 ml) water

MAKE THE FILLING: Slice the onions into thin ¼-inch (6-mm) round slices. In a frying pan over medium heat, melt the butter and cook the onions until very browned and less than a quarter in size, about 40 minutes. Meanwhile, on a cast-iron flat grill or skillet, sear the meat over high heat to brown and cook through. Add the onions and banana peppers to the meat and cook together for about 3 minutes. Remove from the heat and allow to cool. Mix in the cheese.

STUFF IT!: To form the dumplings, get your filling and wonton wrappers ready, along with a little cup of water. Spoon a nice heaping tablespoon (15 g) of the mixture onto each wonton wrapper. Lightly wet the edges of the wrapper and fold it onto itself to form a triangle.

COOK IT: Get a thin layer of oil in a pan over medium-high heat. Add about 8 pot stickers at a time. You will notice that they stick. Let them cook for about 3 to 5 minutes to brown the bottom. Add the water and cover quickly. Allow to steam for 3 more minutes. Uncover and the pot stickers should have freed themselves from the bottom of the pan. Remove from the heat and repeat with the next batch.

Peruvian Arroz Tapado

MAKES: 6 SERVINGS
HEAT: 0.3
PIG-OUT SCALE: 4.2

2 cups (330 g) basmati rice
2 medium sweet potatoes

FILLING

1 tablespoon (15 ml) olive oil
1 pound (454 g) ground beef
1 medium onion, diced
1 green bell pepper, seeded and diced
3 cloves garlic, minced
1 tablespoon (6 g) smoked paprika
2 teaspoons cumin
1 (28-ounce [784-g]) can diced tomatoes (I like Muir Glen)
3 hard-boiled eggs, chopped
¼ cup (16 g) chopped parsley
¼ cup (25 g) chopped black olives

A few years back I had a really good friend from Peru and it helped me get into the world of Peruvian cuisine. Now Peruvian food is suddenly front and center of all the popular food trends of the world. This dish, which translates to "covered rice," is as simple as making a hearty beef filling and mounding cooked rice around it. It's very common in Peru, and each household has its own version.

MAKE THE RICE: Put a pot of salted water on the stove to boil as if you were going to cook pasta. Cook the rice in the pot like pasta, boiling until tender and then straining.

MAKE THE POTATOES: Preheat the oven to 450°F (230°C, or gas mark 8). Cut the potatoes into about 1-inch (2.5-cm) chunks and season with salt and pepper. Roast until tender.

MAKE THE FILLING: In a large frying pan with a little bit of olive oil, cook the beef until browned and cooked through. Remove from the pan and drain most of the excess fat, but leave a few tablespoons' (30 ml) worth in the pan. Add the onion and pepper to the pan and cook for about 10 minutes, until just beginning to brown. Add the garlic and cook for 1 minute. Add the paprika and cumin and stir to combine. Add the meat back to the pan along with the tomatoes, eggs, parsley and olives. Simmer for about 15 minutes, stirring often to mix well. Finally, add the roasted sweet potatoes and mix until heated through.

STUFF IT!: Depending on what size bowls you are using for a mold, the amount of rice and meat you use will vary. Generally, it's best to do individual-size bowls. Grease the inside of the bowl and add rice to the bottom to about one-third of the way up the side. Press down in the middle of the rice so it forms a nice cavity to put extra filling in. Next, add the meat filling for the middle one-third. Fill with rice to the top of the bowl and press down to make sure everything is tight. Place a serving plate upside down on top of the bowl, and flip the whole thing. Slowly remove the bowl and you should have a perfect mound of rice and beef.

Lasagna Timpano

MAKES: 6 TO 8 SERVINGS
HEAT: 1.1
PIG-OUT SCALE: 7.6

PESTO

2 cups (120 g) basil leaves

½ cup (50 g) grated Parmesan

¼ cup (35 g) pine nuts

2 cloves garlic

1 teaspoon pepper

¼ cup (60 ml) olive oil

LASAGNA

2 pounds (908 g) lasagna noodles

1 cup (235 ml) Cream Sauce (page 195)

10 slices salami

2 cups (230 g) shredded mozzarella

15 slices provolone

1 cup (100 g) shredded Parmesan

2 cups (250 g) Meaty Tomato Sauce (page 193)

2 cups (450 g) ricotta

I went to see tUnE-yArDs on a Monday night with some friends, and as always we wanted to cook a meal that somehow related to the show we were heading to. Sometimes this is hard to do, but other times it seems to come naturally. Finding culinary inspiration in Merrill's lyrics seemed like it would be tough, but my sister knew what she wanted to make without hesitation. "How about something layered, because of all the vocal and instrument layering in the music?" From there we worked together to come up with this deep, colorful and multi-flavored lasagna version of a timpano. If you are using words like deep, colorful and multi-flavored to describe something inspired by tUnE-yArDs, you already know you got it right!

This recipe instantly became the most popular and most requested post on my website and remains at the top today. It's a lot easier to make than it seems, and it's crazy impressive-looking, colorful and most of all, flavorful.

• •

MAKE THE PESTO: Put all the pesto ingredients into the food processor and pulse until smooth.

STUFF IT!: Blanch your lasagna noodles in salted boiling water. Slightly undercook them so that they don't become too soggy after baking. Once you have your sauces and ingredients ready, the hardest part of this recipe is actually forming the outside layer. You might want to enlist a friend's help. Lightly grease the bowl first, then start with a single lasagna noodle that goes from the bottom center of the bowl and hangs over the edge. Continue to add noodles, overlapping them slightly so that they fan out from the center and making sure that they are pressed against the side of the bowl.

Once the outside layer is intact, it's just like making any lasagna. Get some cream sauce in the bottom, along with a layer of salami and a blend of mozzarella, provolone and Parm, then put down your first layer of noodles. Keep the first third of the timpano cream sauce, cheese blend and salami, but be sure to reserve a few tablespoons of the cream sauce. Put down another layer of noodles. The middle third should be layers of pesto and the cheese blend, then another layer of noodles. The last third should be meat sauce and ricotta. Keep things somewhat dry inside the timpano so that it doesn't completely fall apart when you cut into it.

Finally, when you get to the top of the bowl, put down your final layer of noodles and press down lightly to make sure everything is nice and secure and tight. Grab that reserved cream sauce and lightly brush it onto the top lasagna layer. Fold the noodles that are hanging over the edge of the bowl onto the top lasagna layer and brush on some more of the cream sauce to serve as a glue. Make sure everything is sealed up tight.

COOK IT: Preheat the oven to 350°F (180°C, or gas mark 4). Bake for about an hour and 15 minutes. When you take it out of the oven, let it rest for a solid 20 minutes before you attempt the flip.

When ready to serve, put a nice sturdy baking sheet or a cutting board on top of the bowl. Grab the bowl and the cutting board, holding them together tightly, and flip the whole thing. Put it on the table and slowly and gently lift the bowl off the timpano, giving it gentle nudges and shakes if needed. Slice the timpano into nice pie slices and serve with any extra sauce.

Spaghetti Wrapped Shrimp

I've eaten variations on this idea a few times in my life, but for some reason I can't find any evidence of it on the web. I was trying to do research on it, see what to call it, where it was originated or which restaurants serve it, but I always came up short. Regardless, it's a fun little trick and a neat way to serve shrimp that looks elegant but is really easy.

MAKES: 24 SHRIMP
HEAT: 0.9
PIG-OUT SCALE: 5.1

SHRIMP AND PASTA

24 shrimp
1 pound (454 g) spaghetti
Vegetable oil, for frying

DIPPING SAUCE

½ cup (112 g) butter
1 teaspoon garlic powder
1 teaspoon red pepper flakes

PREPARE THE SHRIMP AND PASTA: Clean and devein the shrimp, removing the shell but leaving the tail (or just buy them that way). In a pot of salted boiling water, cook the pasta until al dente, and then drain. After you drain the pasta, do not rinse or toss in oil. The sticky nature of the noodles will help them wrap around the shrimp.

MAKE THE DIPPING SAUCE: Melt the butter in a small microwave-safe bowl, then stir in the garlic and red pepper flakes.

STUFF IT!: Grab about 15 strands of pasta. Straighten them out in your hand as best you can and use them like a rope to wrap around one shrimp. Don't kill yourself trying to make them perfect. Use the sticky pasta to help keep everything in place, and set it down on a plate or pan. Repeat until you complete all the shrimp.

COOK IT: Fill a heavy-bottomed pot with vegetable oil and use a thermometer to monitor the temperature. Bring the oil to 350°F (180°C) and fry the shrimp until they are cooked and the pasta is lightly browned, about 2½ minutes. Remove from the oil and place on a rack to dry. Serve with the sauce.

Pork Stuffed Honey Mustard Arancini

Arancini is always fun to make when you have leftover risotto, but it really gets interesting when you are making the risotto specifically to use in arancini. This means you can really start playing with the flavor combinations, two examples of which I have here. Both of these risottos actually taste great as is, but when you combine them with the fillings and deep-fry them, it becomes incredible.

MAKES: 20 ARANCINI
HEAT: 0
PIG-OUT SCALE: 8.3

RISOTTO

1 teaspoon yellow mustard seed
1 teaspoon black mustard seed
1 medium onion
1 large carrot
2 cloves garlic
1 tablespoon (15 ml) olive oil
Salt
1 cup (165 g) risotto
1 quart (940 ml) chicken stock
¼ cup (45 g) yellow mustard
¼ cup (80 g) honey
5 ounces (140 g) Swiss cheese, shredded

MEATBALLS

3 scallions
1 clove garlic
½ pound (225 g) ground pork
½ cup (60 g) breadcrumbs
1 teaspoon Worcestershire sauce
½ teaspoon salt

Vegetable oil, for frying
2 cups (240 g) breadcrumbs
1 cup (120 g) flour
2 eggs
Salt

MAKE THE RISOTTO: Coarsely grind the mustard seeds in a spice or coffee grinder, or mortar and pestle. Dice the onion and the carrot, and mince the garlic. In a heavy-bottomed saucepan or Dutch oven, heat the olive oil over medium heat and sauté the onion and carrot with a pinch of salt. Cook for about 12 minutes. Add the garlic and cook for 1 minute. Add the risotto and stir well to coat the rice with the oil and lightly toast, about 2 minutes. Add the mustard seeds, then start adding the chicken stock about ½ cup (120 ml) at a time. When the rice looks dry, add a little more until you reach about 3½ cups (823 ml) used. Taste the rice to see if it is tender and keep going if it is not. When it is ready, add the mustard and honey and allow the last of the extra liquid to evaporate. Remove from the heat, add the cheese and stir until it is melted. Allow to cool for a few hours if not overnight.

MAKE THE MEATBALLS: Clean and dice the scallions. Grate the garlic with a microplane. Mix all the meatball ingredients in a large bowl. Roll into 20 mini meatballs, about 1 inch (2.5 cm) in diameter. Pan-fry the meatballs in a splash of oil to cook through, stirring often, about 10 minutes.

STUFF IT!: Set up your fry station by putting the breadcrumbs, flour and eggs in 3 separate shallow bowls. Whisk the eggs. Get the meatballs and risotto out. The risotto should be pretty hard by now. Grab a clump of risotto about 3 tablespoons' (45 g) worth and stick a meatball into it. Form the risotto into a ball around it. Dust with the flour and roll it again with your hands just to make sure everything is pretty sturdy. Lightly flour again, then coat with the egg, then the breadcrumbs. Press the breadcrumbs into the risotto ball really well so they stay attached when frying. Prep batches of 4 or 5 before frying them.

COOK IT: Bring about 3 inches (7.5 cm) of oil to 350°F (180°C) in your Dutch oven. Fry until browned, and if you see any filling leaking out, it's done. Put the fried arancini on a rack or paper towels and lightly salt. Serve immediately.

Buffalo Chicken Stuffed Blue Cheese Arancini

MAKES: 20 ARANCINI
HEAT: 6.1
PIG-OUT SCALE: 8.3

RISOTTO

1 large carrot

1 celery stalk

1 medium onion

2 cloves garlic

1 tablespoon (15 ml) olive oil

1 cup (165 g) risotto

1 quart (940 ml) chicken stock

5 ounces (140 g) crumbled blue cheese

Salt

CHICKEN

2 tablespoons (28 g) butter

½ pound (225 g) boneless, skinless chicken thighs

1 clove garlic, grated

1 habanero pepper, minced

1 teaspoon red pepper flakes

¼ cup (60 ml) cayenne sauce

1½ teaspoons honey

Salt

Vegetable oil, for frying

2 cups (230 g) breadcrumbs

1 cup (120 g) flour

2 eggs

Eating dinner once at a classy steakhouse, I was having trouble enjoying a nice blue cheese risotto. It was really delicious, and so was the steak it came with, but I just couldn't stop thinking about how good it would taste with buffalo chicken! I brought the leftovers home and made these arancini the next day.

• •

MAKE THE RISOTTO: Dice the carrot, celery, and onion, and mince the garlic. In a heavy-bottomed saucepan or Dutch oven, heat some olive oil over medium heat and sauté the veggies for about 8 minutes. Add the garlic and cook for 1 minute. Add the risotto and stir well to coat the rice with oil and lightly toast, about 2 minutes. Start adding the chicken stock about ½ cup (120 ml) at a time. When the rice looks dry, add a little more until you reach about 3½ cups (820 ml) used. Taste the rice to see if it is tender and keep going if it is not, adding the remaining ½ cup (120 ml) stock. Allow the last of the extra liquid to evaporate and remove from the heat. Add the cheese and stir until melted. Season with salt, if needed. Allow to cool for a few hours if not overnight.

MAKE THE CHICKEN: In a frying pan, melt the butter and throw in the chicken. Cook over medium heat for about 10 minutes, lightly browning. Add the garlic, habanero and red pepper flakes and mix well. Add the cayenne sauce and honey continue to simmer for another 10 to 15 minutes, until the chicken is very tender. Shred and break up the chicken right there in the pan with a wooden spoon. Taste and add more red pepper flakes if you want it spicier. Season with salt if needed, but depending on the brand and type of butter and cayenne sauce you are using, it may be salty enough. Remove from the heat and let cool.

STUFF IT!: Set up your frying station by putting the breadcrumbs, flour and eggs in 3 separate shallow bowls. Whisk the eggs. Get the chicken and risotto out. The risotto should be pretty hard by now. Grab a clump of risotto about 3 tablespoons' (45 g) worth and form it into a ball. Use your thumb to make an impression and stuff a nice hefty tablespoon of chicken into the hole. Form the risotto into a ball around it. Dust with the flour and roll it again with your hands just to make sure everything is pretty sturdy. Lightly flour again, then coat with the egg, then the breadcrumbs. Press the breadcrumbs into the risotto ball really well so they stay attached when frying. Prep batches of 4 or 5 before frying them.

COOK IT: Bring about 3 inches (7.5 cm) of oil to 350°F (180°C) in your Dutch oven. Fry until browned and if you see any filling leaking out, it's done. Put the fried arancini on a rack or paper towels and lightly season with salt. Serve immediately.

Lobster Stuffed Fried Mac and Cheese Balls

This is the same idea as arancini, but instead of rice, it uses mac and cheese. It's a riff on the insanely popular trend of lobster mac and cheese, but puts it all into a nice little bite. The key to this recipe, as with many lobster-macs, is the delicate balance of the cheese and lobster with the rest of the ingredients, so as not to overpower the delicate lobster flavor.

MAKES: 20 BALLS
HEAT: 0
PIG-OUT SCALE: 8.3

FILLING

8 ounces (225 g) lobster meat
¼ cup (60 g) mayonnaise
1 tablespoon (3 g) chopped chives
1 ½ teaspoons chopped tarragon
½ cup (80 g) chopped tomatoes

MAC AND CHEESE

½ small onion
1 clove garlic
8 ounces (225 g) Cheddar cheese
8 ounces (225 g) Monterey Jack cheese
½ pound (225 g) pasta
1½ tablespoons (21 g) butter
1½ tablespoons (12 g) flour
1½ cups (355 ml) milk
Salt
2 tablespoons (30 ml) truffle oil

Vegetable oil, for frying
2 cups (230 g) breadcrumbs
1 cup (120 g) flour
2 eggs

MAKE THE FILLING: Combine the lobster, mayonnaise, chives, tarragon and tomato in a bowl. Set aside in the fridge until needed.

MAKE THE MAC: Dice the onion very small. Mince the garlic. Grate the cheese. Bring water to a boil in a pot and cook your pasta according to package directions. Meanwhile, cook the onion in the butter for about 5 minutes. Toss in the garlic. Next add the flour and whisk well to combine. Cook for about 3 minutes, stirring the whole time, until the flour turns a slightly toasted hue. Add the milk and whisk well to eliminate any lumps. Bring to a simmer and remove from the heat. Add the pasta, then mix in the cheeses. Stir until all the cheese melts, which should happen naturally, but you can put it back over low heat if necessary. Taste and add salt if necessary, as all cheese has different salt contents. Stir in the truffle oil. Grease 2 mini muffin tins and spoon the mac and cheese into the 24 spaces. As the pasta cools, it will become more solid and moldable, so you may want to wait a few minutes before you start this step.

STUFF IT!: Squeeze a pinch of the lobster mixture into the center of the pasta. Add a little more pasta to the top if the lobster is sticking out a little. Allow these to cool in the fridge for at least 2 hours if not overnight.

FRY 'EM UP: Bring about 3 inches (7.5 cm) of oil to 350°F (180°C) in your Dutch oven. Meanwhile, set up your frying station by putting the breadcrumbs, flour and eggs in 3 separate shallow bowls. Whisk the eggs. Grab the mac and cheese out of the fridge and start popping the individual mac and cheese rounds out of the muffin tin. One by one, lightly flour, then coat with the egg, then the breadcrumbs. Press the breadcrumbs into the mac and cheese really well so they stay attached when frying. Prep batches of 4 or 5 before frying them. Fry until browned and if you see any filling leaking out, it's done. Put the fried mac and cheese onto a rack or paper towels and lightly season with salt. Serve immediately.

Chicken Coconut Sticky Rice with Mango Purée

MAKES: 5 RICE BALLS
HEAT: 2.4
PIG-OUT SCALE: 4.3

The best thing about mango is that it forms this beautiful sauce simply by putting it into the blender or food processor. No other fruit or veggie can form a sauce like that without any assistance. The mango sauce is a perfect dip for these sticky, sweet rice balls with their sharp, salty chicken filling.

MAKE THE CHICKEN: Season the chicken with salt and sear on both sides in a hot pan with some oil. Lower the heat and add the garlic, ginger, Sriracha, soy sauce and sesame oil. Cover and cook over low heat until the chicken is cooked through, about 20 minutes. Chop and shred the chicken and mix well with the cooked sauce.

MAKE THE RICE: Soak the rice in the water for 30 to 60 minutes. Put the rice along with the soaking liquid into a small saucepan and add the coconut milk. Bring to a simmer, and cook for about 20 minutes, until the liquid is absorbed. Unlike normal rice cooking, leave the cover only halfway on the pot to allow steam to escape.

MAKE THE SAUCE: Peel and pit the mangoes and toss the flesh into a food processor. Season with salt and pepper and process until smooth.

STUFF IT!: When the rice is cooked, grab some in the palm of your hand, put a nice big clump of chicken in the center, and wrap the rice around it. The rice balls should be about 2 inches (5 cm) in diameter. Pour some black sesame seeds onto a plate and roll the rice ball in them to decorate the outside of the ball. Serve with the mango purée as a dipping sauce.

CHICKEN

1 large boneless, skinless chicken breast

Salt

1 tablespoon (15 ml) vegetable oil

1 clove garlic, grated

1-inch (2.5-cm) piece ginger, grated

1 tablespoon (15 ml) Sriracha

3 tablespoons (45 ml) soy sauce

2 tablespoons (30 ml) sesame oil

RICE

1 cup (165 g) glutinous or sweet rice

1¼ cups (295 ml) water

1 (14-ounce [400-ml]) can coconut milk

SAUCE

3 mangoes

Salt and pepper

Black sesame seeds, for garnish

vii. Ground beef

FLAVORED
EXTRA VIRGIN
OLIVE OIL
White
Truffle

Net Content
250 ml ℮ (8.5 fl.oz.)

vi. Truffle oil

v. Cooked french fr

i. Parmesan

iv. Lettuce

ii. Black pepper

iii. Tomato slices

CHAPTER 3:

StuffeD Meats

You can get really creative when stuffing meats. Stuffing meat means flank steak roll-ups, stuffed burgers and stuffed squid. Even stuffed eggs! There is a turkey in here too. I take the bones right out and fill it up with loads of duck and chicken and sausage cornbread stuffing. This section is also home to one of my most famous, or infamous, recipes—the mac and cheese stuffed burger.

Mac and Cheese Stuffed Burger

MAKES: 8 BURGERS
HEAT: 0
PIG-OUT SCALE: 8.8

There isn't a single recipe out there that sums up my cooking style better than this one. Take two things you love, combine them in a unique way, and end up with something better than the sum of its parts. In this case, we have two crowd favorites, the burger and mac and cheese, both made from simple ingredients and techniques. If you just smother a burger with a big scoop of mac and cheese, it would be good, and it would be fun, but it would still be a burger with mac and cheese. Putting the pasta into the center of the burger is what really makes this dish special.

• •

MAC AND CHEESE

½ small onion

1 clove garlic

8 ounces (225 g) Cheddar cheese

8 ounces (225 g) Monterey Jack cheese

8 ounces (225 g) pasta

1½ tablespoons (21 g) butter

1½ tablespoons (12 g) flour

1½ cups (355 ml) milk

Salt

2.25 lb (1 kg) beef

Salt and pepper

1 cup (120 g) breadcrumbs

¼ cup (60 ml) olive oil

20 tomato slices

8 burger buns

MAKE THE MAC AND CHEESE: Dice the onion very small. Mince the garlic. Grate the cheeses. Bring a pot of salted water to a boil and cook your pasta until al dente according to package directions. Meanwhile, cook the onion in the butter for about 5 minutes. Toss in the garlic. Next, add the flour and whisk well to combine. Cook for about 3 minutes, stirring the whole time, until the flour turns a slightly toasted hue. Add the milk and whisk well to eliminate any lumps. Bring to a simmer and remove from the heat. Add the pasta, then mix in the cheese. Stir until all the cheese melts, which should happen naturally, but you can put it back on to low heat if necessary. Taste and add salt if necessary, as all cheeses have different salt contents. Pour the pasta into a 9 x 13-inch (23 x 33 cm) pan lined with parchment paper and smooth out into a thin layer. Refrigerate until hardened, about 2 hours.

Cut your sheet of mac and cheese into rounds about 3¼ inches (8.3 cm) in diameter to facilitate burgers that will be 4 to 4½ inches (10 to 11.4 cm) round. A cookie cutter will help with this task if you have one that is the right size. You should be able to get 10 or 11 mac and cheese patties out of this if you cut it right.

STUFF IT!: Roll your beef out thin (about ½ inch [1.3 cm]) and lightly season with salt and pepper. Place a mac and cheese round onto the beef and wrap the pasta in the meat. Tightly seal and press out any air.

Mix the breadcrumbs with the olive oil. Lay your tomatoes on a sheet pan and press some breadcrumbs onto each tomato round. Broil the tomatoes for a minute or two to brown the breadcrumbs.

COOK IT: Grill your burgers for about 7 minutes per side, being sure to close the grill or cover the burgers so that the pasta inside is heated through. If you see any cheese starting to explode out of the burger, take it off the grill. Build the burger by putting one of the patties on the bottom bun, topping with two breadcrumb-coated tomato slices and then the top bun.

Frank-in-burger

MAKES: 1 FRANK-IN-BURGER
HEAT: 0
PIG-OUT SCALE: 8.6

¼ pound (112 g) or less ground beef
1 hot dog
1 slice bacon
1 hot dog bun
Mustard
Slice of onion

The frank-in-burger is a mashup of a burger and a hot dog, with some bacon thrown in for good measure. The idea came to me just as obviously as you may have thought it did . . . I couldn't decide whether I wanted a burger or a hot dog on a lazy afternoon. I did what I usually do in this situation, and instead of eating both I put them together as one.

• •

STUFF IT!: Flatten the ground beef with your palm to form a rectangle. You want it pretty thin. Place the hot dog on top of the beef rectangle. Wrap the beef around the dog and secure it. Leave the ends open. Microwave the bacon for about 45 seconds. This is going to get the bacon started cooking so it crisps up on the burger before the whole thing becomes overcooked and dried out. Finally, wrap the bacon around the beef in a spiral. It should adhere to itself without much trouble.

COOK IT: Put the ends of the bacon side down on the grill first just to help them stay better. Grill the frank-in-burger on all sides until the bacon is crispy, the meat is cooked and dog is heated through, about 10 to 15 minutes on medium heat. Serve on the bun with the mustard and onion.

Queso Fundido Stuffed Burger

MAKES: 4 BURGERS
HEAT: 7.3
PIG-OUT SCALE: 9.1

The Juicy Lucy is a staple in Minneapolis, where the slogan is literally "fear the cheese" because the cheese stuffed inside the burger gets so hot that when people bite into the burger it just comes oozing out and burns you in the face. I wanted to take this idea up a notch so that you feared the cheese not only because it was burning hot, but also because it was spicy! I took inspiration from the Mexican cheese dip queso fundido for the filling.

FILLING

1 chorizo sausage, diced small

1 small onion, diced

1 clove garlic, minced

2 cups (300 g) grated chihuahua cheese (low-moisture mozzarella will work as a substitute)

1 tablespoon (4 g) red pepper flakes

BURGERS

1¼ pounds (568 g) ground beef

2 poblano peppers

4 buns

MAKE THE FILLING: Sauté the chorizo in a hot pan with the onion until they both begin to brown. Add the garlic for just a minute and then remove from the heat. Allow to cool slightly, then toss in a bowl with the cheese and red pepper flakes.

STUFF IT!: Divide the beef into 8 equal pieces. On a sheet of waxed paper, lay the beef out and press flat. Put one-fourth of your cheese mixture in the center of 4 of the patties and press down really well. Top with the remaining 4 patties and press the middle down to remove a bit of the air. Press the edges tightly together. Refrigerate the burgers until you are ready to grill.

COOK IT: Get your poblano peppers on the grill and blacken the skin. Put them into a paper bag while you cook the burgers. Grill your burgers for about 8 to 10 minutes per side, being very watchful of cheese leakage. When the burgers are done, allow them to cool for 5 minutes. While the burgers cool, get the poblanos out of the bag and peel off most of the skin. Cut the peppers in half and remove the seeds. Put the burger on the bun and top with the poblano slice.

Parmesan Truffle French Fry StuffeD Burger

MAKES: 4 BURGERS
HEAT: 0
PIG-OUT SCALE: 9.2

Having to pause from eating a juicy and flavorful burger to grab some french fries seems like such a tedious task to me. How have we as a society not yet found a better way? Enter the Fry Stuffed Burger! And not just any fries, but the classiest of all fries. Don't bother going through all the work to make crispy delicious homemade french fries for this burger, because frozen will work just fine.

. . . .

FRENCH FRIES

About 40 store-bought frozen french fries

¼ cup (25 g) grated Parmesan cheese

2 teaspoons black pepper

1 to 2 tablespoons (15 to 30 ml) truffle oil

Salt

BURGERS

1¼ pounds (568 g) ground beef

4 slices cheese

Ketchup

4 burger buns

4 tomato slices

Lettuce

MAKE THE FRIES: Cook the french fries according to package instructions. Mix the Parm, black pepper and truffle oil in a large bowl with some salt. While still hot, put the fries into the bowl and toss to coat.

STUFF IT!: Divide the beef into 4 equal pieces. On a sheet of waxed paper, lay the beef out and press flat, forming a long patty. Place about 10 french fries on the patty the short way so that some of the ends are hanging over the edge of the meat. Fold the beef over the fries so that you end up with a burger-size piece of meat that is essentially wrapped around the fries with some fries sticking out the sides. Really press the meat into the fries to form a tight patty.

COOK IT: Grill your burgers for 8 to 10 minutes per side and top with the cheese. Build the burger by putting ketchup on the bottom bun, topping with the patty, and followed by the tomato and lettuce and then the top bun.

Salami Arugula Braciole

MAKES: 8 TO 10 SERVINGS
(OR MORE IF EATING WITH PASTA)
HEAT: 0
PIG-OUT SCALE: 6.8

2 pounds (908 g) flank steak

Salt

½ pound (225 g) sliced salami

½ cup (50 g) grated Parmesan cheese

1 cup (115 g) breadcrumbs

3 cups (60 g) arugula

1 recipe Meaty Tomato Sauce
(page 193)

1 pound (454 g) pasta, or as needed

Growing up, I knew that any time a braciole was in the saucepot it was going to be a special dinner. We ate pasta with meat sauce about once a week, but when there was a huge hunk of meat in the sauce it meant there were guests coming over. And for good reason—cooking a flank steak down for hours in a hearty tomato sauce creates a really tender and flavorful piece of meat! This is a twist I put on the recipe that includes savory salami and peppery arugula.

. . . .

PREP THE STEAK: On a cutting board, use your hand to secure the steak from the top and run your knife through the steak between your hand and the cutting board, but don't go all the way through. The seam that you leave should be going with the grain of the steak. Open the steak like a book. Cover it with plastic wrap and pound it out just to thin it a little.

STUFF IT!: Season the meat with salt and start laying the salami onto it. Top with the cheese, breadcrumbs and then the arugula. Tightly roll into a spiral and secure with twine. The grain of the meat should run from end to end, not spiraled in the roll. Put the roll into a baking dish, and ladle on your meat sauce.

COOK IT: Preheat the oven to 325°F (170°C, or gas mark 4). Cover and bake for 2½ hours. In a pot of salted water, cook the pasta according to package directions and then drain. Mix it with the sauce from the baking dish. Slice the meat into pinwheels and serve. It is important that the meat is cut correctly (against the grain) to be tender.

Cuban-Influenced German Rouladen

MAKES: 8 TO 10 SERVINGS
(OR MORE IF EATING WITH PASTA)
HEAT: 0
PIG-OUT SCALE: 6.8

2 pounds (908 g) flank steak

Salt

6 tablespoons (66 g) Dijon mustard

3 pickles, sliced

1 onion, sliced

12 slices Swiss cheese

6 large slices ham

4 oranges

Beef stock

This dish is like the braciole of Germany, a similarly rolled piece of flank steak wrapped up and baked until tender. The German version is very close to having all the flavors of a Cuban sandwich, so I just added a few tweaks to make it complete.

• •

PREP THE STEAK: If you have a really large flank steak, cut it in half against the grain of the meat.

On a cutting board, use your hand to secure the steak from the top and run your knife through the steak between your hand and the cutting board, slicing it into 3 thin sheets. Repeat with the other half. The thinner half might only be able to cut into 2 sheets.

STUFF IT!: Season the steaks with salt and spread about 1 tablespoon (11 g) mustard on each. Next, add the pickles, onion, 2 slices of cheese and 1 slice of ham evenly to the meat. Tightly roll into spirals and secure with twine or skewers. The grain of the meat should run from end to end, not spiraled in the roll. Put the rolls into a baking dish and juice the oranges over them. Add enough beef stock to come about ½ inch (1.3 cm) up the sides of the steak.

COOK IT: Preheat the oven to 300°F (150°C, or gas mark 2). Cover and bake for 1½ hours, flipping once during cooking. Slice into pinwheels and serve. It is important that the meat is cut correctly (against the grain) to be tender.

Meat Wrapped Corn on the Cob

MAKES: 4 CORN

HEAT: 0.7

PIG-OUT SCALE: 5.8

This dish was the huge surprise of all the recipe testing for this cookbook. I was brainstorming with some friends at a restaurant about any ideas they might have for fun stuffed foods. At the time we happened to be eating corn on the cob, a food that I had totally written off for any stuffing-related idea, when my friend said, "Hey, what if you just wrapped ground beef around a corn on the cob?" I laughed the idea off, but a few days later I happened to have a few cobs of corn, a pound of ground beef and the hunger for something new.

I tried to put the beef on the corn and it fell right off, so, feeling defeated and lazy, I wrapped the whole mess in plastic wrap and popped it into the fridge. A few hours later I noticed that the beef had firmed up! I got it into the oven and as the beef cooked, it almost shrink-wrapped to the corn! I was able to eat it just as we had initially envisioned—like a meat and corn version of a candy apple.

• •

MEAT MIXTURE

1¼ pounds (568 g) ground beef

1 bunch scallions, minced

1 clove garlic, minced

2 eggs

½ cup (50 g) shredded Parmesan

1 teaspoon salt

1 tablespoon (6 g) freshly ground black pepper

1 tablespoon (15 ml) Worcestershire sauce

4 cobs of corn, cleaned, with the stem still intact about 2 inches (5 cm) long

MASHED POTATO DIP

1 large russet potato

½ teaspoon salt

Olive oil

4 tablespoons (56 g) butter, melted

1 cup (225 g) cream cheese

1 cup (235 ml) milk

1 cup (115 g) shredded Cheddar cheese

1 teaspoon freshly ground black pepper

MAKE THE MEAT MIXTURE: Combine all of the meat ingredients in a large bowl. Divide the mixture into 4 equal parts. Lay each portion onto a sheet of plastic wrap and press it flat into a rectangle shape. Lay the corn on top and use the plastic wrap to wrap the meat around the corn. Seal it up and make sure the whole thing is wrapped well except for the stem. Put it into the fridge for at least an hour.

MAKE THE POTATO DIP: Preheat the oven to 350˚F (180˚C, or gas mark 4). Rub the potato with oil and season with salt. Bake for about 1 hour, or until tender. Peel and mash with the rest of the ingredients. Microwave the mixture for a minute if it's too cold or the cheese won't melt fully and continue to mix. Serve warm.

ROAST THE CORN: Turn up the oven to 450˚F (230˚C, or gas mark 8). Remove the plastic wrap from the corn. Roast the meat-covered corn for about 25 minutes, until fully cooked. If you want to grill the corn, that works too, but you need to be very gentle handling it, and make sure it is cold when it gets on the grill, the grill is nicely greased and it is evenly cooked on all sides. It should also take about 25 minutes.

Chicken Parm Stuffed Meatballs

This is another one of those "which one do I want" type dishes. When you can't decide between two things, sometimes combining them into something new is the best option!

CHICKEN

1 boneless, skinless chicken breast

Salt and pepper

1 egg

½ cup (60 g) flour

1 cup (115 g) breadcrumbs

½ cup (50 g) grated Parmesan cheese

Vegetable oil, for frying

MEATBALLS

2 cloves garlic

¼ cup (60 ml) milk

2 slices white bread or any leftover bread

1 large egg

¼ cup (16 g) chopped parsley

½ pound (225 g) ground beef

½ pound (225 g) ground turkey

¼ cup (25 g) finely grated Parmesan cheese

1 teaspoon salt

PREPARE THE CHICKEN: Slice the chicken the long way to form 2 thinner cutlets. One by one, lay down a sheet of plastic wrap, then cover the chicken with another sheet and lightly pound it out to thin it even further. Remove the plastic, and season with salt and pepper.

Whisk up the egg, and put the egg, flour and breadcrumbs into 3 separate dishes. Mix the Parm into the breadcrumbs. Dredge the chicken in the flour, followed by the egg and then the breadcrumbs. In a frying pan with a ½ inch (1.3 cm) layer of oil, fry the chicken on both sides to brown and cook through, about 7 minutes per side.

MIX THE MEATBALLS: Put the garlic into a food processor and pulse to finely chop. Add the milk, bread, egg and parsley to the food processor and process until well combined. It should look like a thick gray paste with flecks of green. In a large bowl, mix the beef and turkey, and add in your paste, the Parmesan cheese and the salt. Mix gently until well combined.

STUFF IT!: Chop the chicken into 1-inch (2.5-cm) cubes. Get a few tablespoons (30 g) of the meatball mixture and use your palm to flatten it out on your work surface. Place a piece of chicken on the meatball mixture and wrap it around the chicken. Push it tight to remove any air. You should get 25 to 30 meatballs.

COOK IT: Line the meatballs up on a pan, and broil them for about 7 minutes per side until browned and cooked through. Serve these with pasta or in the ultimate meatball/chicken Parm mashup sub.

Panang Rice Stuffed Ginger Chicken Meatballs

MAKES: 20 TO 25 MEATBALLS
HEAT: 8.7
PIG-OUT SCALE: 4.9

Stuffing rice in the center of a meatball is like the opposite of the meatball stuffed arancini on page 92, which is kind of fun to think about. Spicy panang curried rice is a perfect complement to go inside this ginger chicken meatball. These meatballs are good as is with some dipping sauce, but would taste awesome in a banh mi.

. . . .

PANANG CURRY PASTE
(or 2 to 4 tablespoons [22 to 44 g] store-bought)

18 fresh Thai green and red chiles

5 shallots, roughly diced

5 cloves garlic, minced

2 tablespoons (18 g) crushed peanuts

2 tablespoons (12 g) minced lemongrass (just the tender hearts)

1½ teaspoons lime zest

Stems and roots from 1 bunch cilantro

1 tablespoon (6 g) cumin

1 tablespoon (6 g) coriander

1 teaspoon black pepper

1 teaspoon fish sauce

1 tablespoon (15 ml) vegetable oil

RICE FILLING

2 (14-ounce [400-ml]) cans coconut milk

15 kaffir lime leaves

The stringy/woody parts of the lemongrass, broken with the back of a knife

1 cup (165 g) jasmine rice

MEATBALLS

1¼ pounds (568 g) ground chicken

Leaves from 1 bunch cilantro, finely chopped

2-inch (5-cm) piece ginger, grated

1 clove garlic, grated

1 teaspoon red pepper flakes

2 teaspoons fish sauce

MAKE THE PASTE: Remove the seeds from the chilies and then roughly chop them. If you are using whole spices, first grind them in a spice grinder or mortar and pestle, then add everything for the curry paste to a food processor. Blend until smooth.

MAKE THE RICE FILLING: Cook the paste in a hot frying pan with a splash of oil for about 2 minutes, stirring constantly. Add the coconut milk, lime leaves and lemongrass and stir to combine. Bring to a simmer. Add the rice. Simmer and cook, stirring often, until the rice cooks and is tender, about 20 minutes. The rice should absorb most of the liquid in the pan. Taste the rice and season with salt if needed. Allow to cool before stuffing, about an hour.

MAKE THE MEATBALLS: Mix all of the meatball ingredients. Allow this to cool in the fridge while you are waiting for the rice to cool.

STUFF IT!: Take the rice out of the fridge and start forming small balls with it, about 1 inch (2.5 cm) in diameter. Flatten some meat into the palm of your hand, put the rice ball on top of it and wrap the meat around it, adding more if needed. They should end up as large meatballs, around 2 inches (5 cm) in diameter.

COOK IT: Broil the meatballs for about 7 minutes per side, until browned all around and fully cooked through. Serve the meatballs as an appetizer with the Basil-Carrot Raita sauce (page 195), pureéd mango (page 96) or Thai Sweet and Sour Sauce (page 195).

Shepherd's/Cottage Pie Meatballs

MAKES: 30 TO 35 MEATBALLS
HEAT: 0
PIG-OUT SCALE: 6.4

POTATOES

2 large russet potatoes

Olive oil

Salt and pepper

4 tablespoons (56 g) butter

2 carrots, diced

1 small onion, diced

2 cups (230 g) corn

½ cup (120 ml) cream

MEATBALLS

2 cloves garlic, chopped

2 tablespoons (30 ml) Worcestershire sauce

2 slices bread

2 tablespoons (30 ml) milk

¼ cup (16 g) chopped parsley

1 teaspoon salt

1½ pounds (680 g) ground beef or lamb

If you call something shepherd's pie on the Internet but you use beef instead of lamb, people freak out. I personally like this recipe better with beef, but it works both ways, so I wanted to leave it open for you to decide. The fun part of this recipe is biting into a meatball to find the soft mashed potato on the inside!

• •

MAKE THE POTATOES: Preheat the oven to 375°F (190°C, or gas mark 5). Rub the potatoes with oil and season with salt and pepper. Place on a baking sheet and bake for about 1½ hours, until tender.

Meanwhile, heat the butter in a small pan and add the carrot and onion with a pinch of salt. Cook for about 7 minutes, until softened. Add the corn and cook for another 2 minutes. Mix in the cream and remove from the heat. When the potatoes are ready, peel and chop them, put them in a bowl, and pour the corn mixture over them. Mash it up really well. Taste and add salt and pepper if needed.

Allow the potatoes to cool a little, and then begin rolling them into 1-inch (2.5-cm) balls. Put the potato balls onto a baking sheet lined with parchment paper and put them into the freezer for about an hour.

MAKE THE MEATBALLS: Combine the garlic, Worcestershire, bread, milk, parsley and salt in a food processor and pulse until fairly smooth. In a large bowl, mix this mixture into the meat. Refrigerate until ready to use.

STUFF IT!: Take the frozen potato balls out of the freezer and begin wrapping them in meat. Flatten some meat into the palm of your hand, put the potato ball on top of it, and wrap the meat around it, adding more if needed. They should end up as large meatballs, between 2 and 2¼ inches (5 and 5.6 cm) in diameter. Place on a baking sheet.

COOK IT: Broil the meatballs for about 7 minutes per side until browned all around. Keep your eye on potato trying to escape, and if it starts oozing out, get it out of the oven quick! Serve these just as an appetizer with some gravy, or in a meatball sandwich, also with gravy.

Apple Gruyère Stuffed Pork Chop

MAKES: 4 PORK CHOPS
HEAT: 0
PIG-OUT SCALE: 4.8

4 thick-cut pork chops
Salt and pepper
1 apple
½ red onion
4 ounces (112 g) Gruyère cheese
A few sprigs thyme

Most stuffed pork chops are loaded with breadcrumbs and lots of filler. These guys, however, are everything you want in a pork chop. Apple is a natural pairing, and Gruyère and thyme class up the party. This is a super simple recipe that is lots of fun and pays off big-time.

• •

STUFF IT!: Make a horizontal slit in one side of the pork chop. Liberally season the chop, inside and out, with salt and pepper. Make paper-thin slices of the apple, onion and cheese. Take the leaves off the thyme sprigs. Stack the slices in this order: cheese, apple, cheese, onion, thyme, apple, cheese. Make 4 of these stacks, and stuff them into the 4 pork chops.

COOK IT: Grill the chops over medium-high heat until just cooked through and the cheese starts leaking out, about 6 to 7 minutes per side.

Cuban Chicken Cordon Bleu

As you can see, I can't get enough of sticking the Cuban sandwich flavors into other dishes. This version is a really good example of how versatile the flavors are, and how truly delicious this combination can be. I always loved the frozen boxed chicken cordon bleu as a kid, so it was fun to finally make a version of it from scratch!

• •

3 boneless, skinless chicken breasts
Salt and pepper
6 tablespoons (66 g) mustard
6 large slices rosemary ham
12 slices dill pickle
6 slices Swiss cheese

BREADING
2 eggs
1 cup (120 g) flour
2 cups (230 g) breadcrumbs
Vegetable oil, for frying

STUFF IT!: Slice the chicken the long way to form 2 thinner cutlets. One by one, lay down a sheet of plastic wrap, then cover the chicken with another sheet and lightly pound it out to thin it even further. Remove the top piece of plastic, season with salt and pepper and spread each with 1 tablespoon (11 g) mustard, 1 slice of the ham, 2 pickle chips and 1 slice of cheese. Tightly roll up the chicken, using the plastic to help keep it tight. Twist the ends of the plastic to tighten it further and put it into the fridge while you do the rest of them.

BREAD THE CHICKEN: Lightly grease a baking dish. Whisk the eggs, and put the eggs, flour and breadcrumbs into 3 separate dishes. Get the chicken out and stick 2 toothpicks into each chicken to secure it. Gently unwrap the plastic. Dredge the chicken in the flour, followed by the egg and then the breadcrumbs. In a frying pan with a thin layer of oil, working in batches of 2, brown the breadcrumbs onto the chicken on all sides. Transfer the chicken to the baking dish.

COOK IT: Preheat the oven to 350°F (180°C, or gas mark 4). Bake for about 18 minutes, until the chicken is cooked through and no longer pink in the middle.

French Onion Stuffed Fillet

French onion soup is the go-to appetizer at a steakhouse, so I thought, why not stuff it right into the steak? Caramelized onions are pretty much the key to unlocking all the culinary secrets of the world, and when it comes to this steak, it's no different.

• •

MAKES: 4 FILLETS
HEAT: 0
PIG-OUT SCALE: 5.2

FILLING

2 onions, finely diced
1 tablespoon (14 g) butter
A few sprigs thyme
4 ounces (112 g) goat cheese

4 thick beef fillets
Salt and pepper

MAKE THE FILLING: In a skillet over medium heat, sauté the onions in the butter until very browned and drastically reduced in volume, about 25 minutes. Meanwhile, take the leaves off the thyme sprigs. Mix the onions with the goat cheese and add the thyme. Stir well to combine and put the mixture into a piping bag.

STUFF IT!: With a sharp knife, stab one side of the beef fillet. Try and keep the opening the size of the knife, but work the knife back and forth inside the fillet to create a cavity. Take the knife out and spin it around to move in the other direction. Liberally season the fillet with salt and pepper. Pipe the goat cheese mixture evenly into the cavity of the beef.

COOK IT: Grill the chops over medium-high heat until just cooked through and the cheese starts leaking out.

Turducken

MAKES: 20 SERVINGS
HEAT: 2.3
PIG-OUT SCALE: 101

Never in my life did I think I would eat or make a turducken. When I first heard about it thirteen years ago, it sounded gross. But one year I decided to have friends over for Thanksgiving, and they wanted a turducken.

I never imagined how much I would actually enjoy every moment of the process. Sourcing the local birds from farms in the area, deboning a turkey but leaving the right bones so it still looked like a turkey, taking lots of pics, the excitement from friends when they realized that it wasn't a joke anymore. But the best moment was cutting through the turducken in front of the crowd to reveal the meat mass in all its glory, and then of course, devouring it!

• •

STUFFING

4 cups (560 g) crumbled cornbread

1 pound (454 g) loose Italian sausage ('cause if there is anything this dish needs it's a fourth animal)

2 celery sticks, diced

2 carrots, diced

1 onion, diced

2 cloves garlic, minced

1½ cup (225 g) cranberries, roughly chopped

Chicken stock or water, as needed

BRINE

1 cup (290 g) salt

½ cup (100 g) sugar

1 gallon (3.8 L) vegetable stock

1 gallon (3.8 L) ice water

6 to 8 sprigs rosemary

20 allspice berries, crushed

MAKE THE STUFFING: Preheat the oven to 350°F (180°C, or gas mark 4). Place the cornbread in a baking dish and bake for about 15 minutes to lightly toast and dry it out a bit.

Meanwhile, in a skillet over medium heat, cook the sausage until it is very browned, about 10 minutes. Add in the celery, carrots and onion and sauté for another 10 minutes or so. Add the garlic and sauté for 1 minute. Add the cranberries and simmer for about 10 minutes before removing from the heat. Add the cornbread and stir to combine. Pour in a little chicken stock or water if it seems too dry.

MAKE THE BRINE: In a large food-safe bucket, mix together the brine ingredients.

TURDUCKEN

18-pound (8.2 kg) turkey

1 ½ pounds (680 g) boneless, skinless chicken breast

3 to 5 pounds (1362 to 2270 g) boneless, skinless duck breast

GET THE TURKEY READY: Flip the turkey upside down. You want to keep the top of the turkey fully intact for presentational purposes. Use scissors to cut the backbone out of the turkey from the back to the front. Just snip along the edges of the bone on each side to get it out.

The next step is to remove the thigh bones. These are attached to the drumsticks, but we don't want to remove the drumstick, so be careful! Just run your knife along the bone from the inside of the cavity as best as you can, slowly but surely, and you will eventually cut the entire bone out. You then need to crack the joint from the thigh bone to the drumstick to fully remove it.

Finally, you have to get the rib cage out without removing too much of the breasts, or severing the connection at the top of the turkey, which, again, would ruin the whole presentation. Just follow the rib cage with your knife, making shallow but deliberate cuts to free the ribs from the breasts. Add the turkey to the brine and let it sit refrigerated overnight. Once you get through this part, it's all smooth sailing!

ASSEMBLE THE TURDUCKEN: The next day, thinly slice the chicken and duck breasts the long way to form thin cutlets. Slather the cornbread stuffing all over the nooks and crannies of the turkey, which should now be lying on your counter like an open book. Shingle the duck breast on top of the stuffing to form a thin layer. Next, add a little more stuffing. Finally, top with the chicken breast, adding a small amount of stuffing on top. Using kitchen twine, re-form the bird back into a turkey shape by bringing the ends together to the center. Wrap the turkey as tightly as you can. Flip her over and into a roasting dish. Truss the legs and wings.

COOK IT: Preheat the oven to 500°F (250°C, or gas mark 10). Place the roasting pan in the oven and immediately turn it down to 350°F (180°C, or gas mark 4). Roast for about 3½ to 4 hours, until it is fully up to temperature, over 165°F (74°C) in multiple areas. You don't want to mess around with this being at all undercooked.

Kung Pao Stuffed Shrimp

MAKES: 18 SHRIMP
HEAT: 7.8
PIG-OUT SCALE: 4.9

Kung pao shrimp or chicken is my favorite Chinese takeout. Because it isn't breaded I get the illusion that it's slightly better for me than General Gao, even though it's probably not. This recipe takes the kung pao and stuffs it into jumbo shrimp for a unique take on the same flavors. Make sure you cut everything really small because you need the stuffing to be a thick mass and not have huge chunks in it.

FILLING

½ cup (80 g) long-grain rice

2 tablespoons (30 ml) sesame oil, plus more for drizzling

½ cup (80 g) minced onion

¼ cup (30 g) minced celery

3 oranges

2 limes

2 cloves garlic, minced

½ cup (30 g) dried chiles, roughly broken

½ cup (38 g) chopped snap peas

½ cup (75 g) roughly chopped cashews

½ cup (50 g) chopped baby corn

18 jumbo shrimp

MAKE THE FILLING: Put the rice into a spice grinder or mortar and pestle and grind it down so that most of the rice is broken at least in half if not more. Add the oil to a hot skillet and cook the onion and celery for 3 to 5 minutes. Meanwhile, juice the oranges and limes into a cup. Next, add the garlic and chiles to the pan, followed a minute later by the orange and lime juice. Stir in the rice and simmer until the mixture has thickened and the rice is tender, about 20 minutes. Halfway through the rice cooking, add the snap peas. Add a little water if it needs it, but you want the mixture to be thick enough to stuff into the shrimp. When it's just about ready, stir in the cashews and baby corn and remove from the heat.

STUFF IT!: Peel the shrimp and butterfly by slicing down the center along the curve of the shrimp. Cut the shrimp about three-fourths of the way through and devein if you can or need to. Jam about 2 tablespoons (30 g) of the stuffing into the shrimp, making an effort to keep the shrimp looking like shrimp and not just a plate for the stuffing. Lightly grease a baking dish with sesame oil. Place the shrimp on the dish with the stuffing facing upward. Drizzle with a little more sesame oil.

COOK IT: Preheat the oven to 375˚F (190˚C, or gas mark 5). Bake for about 20 minutes, until the shrimp are cooked through.

Vietnamese Pork Stuffed Grilled Squid

MAKES: 10 SQUID HOODS
HEAT: 4.8
PIG-OUT SCALE: 5.2

Squid seems made for stuffing, with its hood almost acting as a sack to collect anything and everything you could imagine stuffing into it. The trouble when figuring out how to stuff a squid is deciding how long to cook it. It is important that squid cooks either very hot and fast, or very low and slow, so the fillings need to follow suit.

• •

FILLING

1 cup (50 g) broken rice stick noodles
½ pound (225 g) ground pork
2 teaspoons fish sauce
2 teaspoons Sriracha
1 teaspoon red pepper flakes
1 teaspoon sugar
½ teaspoon salt
3 scallions, minced
¼ cup (16 g) chopped mint

10 squid hoods, cleaned
Olive oil, for brushing
Thai Sweet and Sour Sauce (page 195)

MAKE THE FILLING: Make sure the noodles are nicely broken up and you have a decent amount of them in the cup measure. Pour some hot water over the noodles and allow them to sit for about 10 minutes before draining and rinsing with cold water. Combine the noodles with all of the remaining filling ingredients.

STUFF AND COOK: Stuff the pork mixture into the squid hoods. Brush with olive oil and grill over low heat with the lid on for about 35 minutes, until the mixture inside is fully cooked. The squid should seem to become rubbery after about 5 minutes of cooking, but then loosen up and become tender again at about the 30-minute mark. Serve with the Thai dipping sauce or chimichurri.

"Rhode Island" Stuffed Squid

This version of stuffed squid uses the quick and hot cooking method. It has a filling that I am calling "Rhode Island" because it has lots of banana peppers, just like the Rhode Island–style fried calamari.

• •

MAKES: 10 SQUID HOODS
HEAT: 6.5
PIG-OUT SCALE: 4.1

MAKE THE FILLING: Preheat the oven to 350°F (180°C, or gas mark 4). Mix the olive oil and breadcrumbs together. Lay them out on a baking sheet and toast in the oven for about 10 minutes, until browned.

In a frying pan, cook the onion in some olive oil for about 5 minutes just to soften. Add the banana and cherry peppers and sauté for 5 minutes over high heat. Add the tomatoes and lower the heat. Mix in the breadcrumbs and remove from the heat.

STUFF AND COOK: Stuff the mixture into the squid hoods. Grill over very high heat for about 5 minutes total, flipping to evenly grill all sides.

FILLING

¼ cup (60 ml) olive oil

1 cup (115 g) panko breadcrumbs

1 onion, diced

1 cup (135 g) chopped pickled banana peppers (with juices)

1 cup (135 g) chopped pickled cherry peppers

1 (14-ounce [392-g]) can diced tomatoes, drained

10 squid hoods, cleaned

Pad Thai Stuffed Squid

Sometimes pad Thai comes with a few little squid pieces floating around in it, so I thought it only natural to stuff squid with pad Thai. This version cooks low and slow in the oven until it passes the point of tender.

MAKES: 15 SQUID HOODS
HEAT: 5.3
PIG-OUT SCALE: 4.9

TAMARIND BROTH

1 box tamarind (about 25 pods)

4 cups (940 ml) chicken stock

FILLING

1 tablespoon (6 g) grated ginger

5 cloves garlic

7 Thai green chiles, seeds removed

6 ounces (168 g) rice stick fettuccini

1 tablespoon (15 ml) vegetable oil

½ pound (225 g) boneless, skinless chicken thighs

4 large carrots, cut into matchsticks

2 eggs, beaten

1 handful bean sprouts

1 bunch scallions

1 tablespoon (15 g) brown sugar

2 limes, juiced

Sriracha

15 squid hoods, cleaned

• •

MAKE THE TAMARIND BROTH: Peel the hard shell off the tamarind pods and place the soft interior into a pot on the stove with the chicken broth. Allow to simmer for about 30 minutes, stirring occasionally. Strain the broth through a fine-mesh strainer, collecting the liquid in a large bowl. Press the tamarind through the strainer to add all the fruit to the broth but leaving the seeds and stringy parts behind in the strainer.

MAKE THE FILLING: Place the ginger, garlic and chiles in a food processor and grind into a paste. Break up the noodles so they aren't as long. Pour boiling water over the noodles and allow to soften for about 5 minutes. Strain and rinse.

Add the oil to a skillet over medium heat, add the chicken and sear on all sides. Remove from the pan. Add the carrots to the pan and sauté for a minute or two, then add the garlic-ginger-chile paste and cook for 1 minute. Add half the tamarind broth and return the chicken to the mix. Simmer for about 20 minutes, until the chicken is cooked through. Remove the chicken and chop into small pieces. Return the chicken to the pot and add a little water if the mixture is too thick.

Bring the liquid to a strong simmer and drizzle in the egg to create pieces of cooked scrambled egg. Remove from the heat and stir in the bean sprouts, scallions, brown sugar, lime juice and Sriracha to taste (1 tablespoon [15 ml] is a good starting point).

STUFF IT!: Stuff the pad Thai mixture into the squid and seal with toothpicks. Spoon a little of the tamarind broth into a baking dish, and then get your squid in there. Pour the rest of the broth over the squid and cover with foil.

COOK IT: Preheat the oven to 350°F (180°C, or gas mark 4). Bake for about 40 minutes.

Banh Mi Deviled Egg

MAKES: 24 DEVILED EGGS
HEAT: 3.9
PIG-OUT SCALE: 7.1

QUICK PICKLED CARROT AND DAIKON

3 carrots

1 small daikon radish

2 cloves garlic, crushed

1½ teaspoons salt

1 teaspoon sugar

2 cups (470 ml) vinegar

PÂTÉ

½ pound (225 g) chicken livers

1 cup (235 ml) milk

1 cup (235 ml) white wine

½ onion, roughly chopped

1 clove garlic, quartered

2 tablespoons (28 g) butter, softened

1 tablespoon (15 ml) fish sauce

12 hard-boiled eggs

GARNISHES

1 cucumber

Cilantro

Sriracha

This twist on deviled eggs is crazy but obvious at the same time. To get the banh mi flavors into the deviled egg, I mixed some freshly made pâté with the egg yolks and sprinkled the final product with pickled carrot and radish and, of course, cilantro.

• •

MAKE THE PICKLES: Use a julienne peeler or a mandoline slicer to make thin strips of the carrot and daikon. Put the carrot and daikon into a jar or bowl with the garlic. Add the salt and sugar to the vinegar and microwave for 2 minutes until very hot. Pour the vinegar mixture over the carrot and daikon and let this mixture sit for at least 2 hours before serving. After the first hour, store it in the fridge.

MAKE THE PÂTÉ: Rinse the chicken livers in cold water, and if you notice any really hard or rough areas, cut it off. Put the livers into a bowl and pour the milk over. Cover and let soak for at least an hour. Strain and discard the milk, and put the chicken livers into a saucepan with the wine, onion and garlic. Bring to a simmer and cook for about 15 minutes. Remove from the heat and allow to cool. Strain and discard the wine, and add the liver and onion mixture to a food processor along with the butter and fish sauce. Crank the food processor to smooth out the mixture as much as you can.

Cut the eggs in half and remove the yolks. Set the whites aside in the refrigerator, and add the yolks to the blender with everything else. When the mixture is as smooth as you can get it, press it through a fine-mesh strainer, to remove any graininess. Pour the mixture into a piping bag, and store it in the fridge for an hour.

STUFF IT!: Line up the egg whites on a serving platter and pipe the pâté mixture into the eggs in a decorative pattern. If the pâté is still really soft, put it back into the fridge for another hour.

Julienne your cucumber and break off small sprigs of cilantro. Decorate each egg with a few pieces of carrot and daikon, a few slices of cucumber, a squirt of Sriracha and a sprig of cilantro. Refrigerate until ready to eat.

Spicy Black Bean Deviled Egg

MAKES: 12 DEVILED EGGS
HEAT: 6.1
PIG-OUT SCALE: 3.9

6 hard-boiled eggs

½ cup (125 g) black beans

½ cup (50 g) chopped scallion, plus more for garnish

¼ cup (34 g) banana peppers, including juice from the jar

Deviled eggs are super trendy right now, and this version is a simple, fun and surprisingly light take on the classic.

• •

Cut the eggs in half and remove the yolk. In a food processor, add the yolks, beans, scallion and banana peppers and juice. Pulse to combine but don't totally purée. Use a piping bag with a decorative tip to pipe your egg yolk mixture into the eggs. When the eggs are all on the serving dish, top with more scallion as garnish.

Scotch Quail Eggs

MAKES: 18 SCOTCH QUAIL EGGS
HEAT: 1.1
PIG-OUT SCALE: 6.4

18 quail eggs

2 chicken eggs

1 cup (120 g) flour

1 cup (115 g) breadcrumbs

Salt

½ pound (225 g) ground beef or loose sausage

Vegetable oil, for frying

Chives, snipped

With the huge popularity of deviled eggs, it surprises me that Scotch eggs haven't surged in popularity as well. They are pretty similar, but instead of messing with the egg yolk, we instead put a totally unique wrapper around the whole egg. What's also fun about Scotch eggs is that with the right attention to detail, we can keep the yolk nice and soft and have no need for a dipping sauce!

• •

COOK THE EGGS: Bring a pot of water to a hard boil. In 3 batches, boil the quail eggs for exactly 1 minute and 50 seconds. Immediately rinse with cold water to stop the cooking process.

Gently peel the eggs, removing the shell and the thin inner shell lining. This is a little tricky if you have never worked with quail eggs before, and I lost 2 or 3 eggs before getting the hang of it. Break the shell all around the egg first, then start at the top, making sure you grab hold of the inner lining as well as the shell. Then work in a spiral around the egg, pulling off the entire shell in one continuous strip.

PREP THE BREADING: Beat the 2 chicken eggs to form an egg wash, and prepare your breading station with a plate of flour, a plate of egg wash and a plate of breadcrumbs. Lightly season the flour and breadcrumbs with salt.

STUFF IT!: Roll out the beef or sausage very thin and season lightly with salt. Lightly flour the eggs. Wrap in a thin layer of meat and press into your hand in an effort to seal the meat all around the egg. Don't press too hard or you will break the yolk! When the meat is sealed around the egg, lightly flour it and roll it around in your hands again, using the flour coating to help seal everything shut. Lightly dust with flour again, then coat in egg wash and then the breadcrumbs.

COOK IT: Deep-fry in batches at 350°F (180°C) for about 2 minutes, until the breadcrumbs are nicely browned. Garnish with the chives and serve.

Pork Stuffed Tofu With Noodles

MAKES: 2 OR 3 SERVINGS
HEAT: 4.6
PIG-OUT SCALE: 4.9

Stuffing meat into tofu is almost like dipping it into a thick batter and frying it. The tofu is so bland on its own and willing to pick up any flavors it is sitting next to that it totally absorbs the flavors from the meat, and forms a crispy layer around it. This version has a flavorful pork filling and is served over noodles almost as if it were a pot sticker.

• •

FILLING

½ pound (225 g) ground pork

2 cloves garlic, grated

¼ onion, grated

1 tablespoon (15 ml) soy sauce

¼ cup (16 g) chopped mint

2 packages firm tofu

Vegetable oil, for frying

SAUCE

2 tablespoons (30 ml) Sriracha

2 tablespoons (30 ml) soy sauce

2 tablespoons (30 ml) gochujang

¼ cup (60 ml) rice vinegar

1 tablespoon (15 ml) brown sugar

NOODLES

1 onion

4 carrots

25 green beans, ends removed and chopped in halves or thirds

1 pound (450 g) chinese noodles

MAKE THE FILLING: Add all the filling ingredients to a bowl and stir to combine.

STUFF AND COOK: Chop the tofu into 1¼-inch (3-cm) squares and dry on paper towels for 30 minutes. Bore out a mini square in each tofu cube. Stuff the pork filling in there. Fry the cubes in a very thin layer of oil for about a minute or two on each side, starting with the open pork side. When you're done, turn off the heat but keep the pan there with the oil.

MAKE THE SAUCE: Mix together the sauce ingredients and stir well.

MAKE THE NOODLES: Thinly slice the carrot and onion. Clean and prep the green beans. Boil the noodles according to the package instructions, and then strain and rinse. Turn the heat back on, and get the onion, carrot and green beans down in the same oil you fried the tofu in. Sauté for about 7 to 8 minutes. Add in the noodles and sauce and mix well. Serve the noodles and top with the tofu.

v. Marscapone

ii. Arugula

i. Black pepper

iii. Peach

iv. Bacon

CHAPTER 4:

Stuffed Veggies and Fruits

Most veggies are pretty much asking to get stuffed. I mean, just look at them! They are mostly roundish, with a cavity in the center. It's really just a question of what's going in there. Well, in this chapter, the answer varies from mac and cheese stuffed into a pepper, to chicken curry stuffed into a mushroom and even bacon stuffed into a peach! We also get into some of the spicier dishes in the book, like my fiery pork and banana habanero peppers that really just blow old-fashioned jalapeño poppers right out of the water!

Mac and Cheese Chile Rellenos

MAKES: 8 STUFFED PEPPERS
HEAT: 5.5
PIG-OUT SCALE: 7.9

MAC AND CHEESE

2 slices bacon
1 clove garlic
¼ cup (35 g) pickled nacho jalapeños
1 tomato
1 tablespoon (15 ml) olive oil
1 small onion, diced
2 cherry peppers, diced
½ pound (225 g) elbow macaroni
2 tablespoons (28 g) butter
1½ tablespoons (21 g) flour
1½ cups (355 ml) milk
½ teaspoon mustard powder
5 ounces (140 g) Cheddar cheese
5 ounces (140 g) Monterey Jack cheese

Vegetable oil
Salt
8 poblano peppers
2 cups (240 g) flour
2 cups (230 g) breadcrumbs
3 eggs, beaten

A chile relleno is normally stuffed with cheese, so why not add some mac in there, too? More traditional chile rellenos have an eggy batter that is almost reminiscent of eating a chile omelet. For this bastardized mac and cheese version, I did the standard American bar food breadcrumb crust and it matched perfectly. These chile rellenos have an amazing balance of crunch, spice, ooze and comfort!

• •

MAKE THE MAC AND CHEESE: Bring a pot of salted water to a boil over high heat. Chop the bacon into ½-inch (1.3-cm) squares. Mince the garlic. Roughly chop the jalapeños and tomatoes.

In a Dutch oven with just a splash of olive oil, cook the bacon until crispy, about 7 minutes, and remove it from the pot. Let drain on paper towels. In the remaining bacon fat, cook the onion and peppers for about 5 minutes, until they start to brown. While the veggies cook, be sure to continually scrape the bottom of the pot to keep the browned bits incorporated with the food and not stuck to the pot. This would be a good time to get your pasta cooking. Add the minced garlic and butter to the onions and peppers and cook for about 2 minutes, until the butter is melted. Mix in the flour and cook, stirring often, until the roux is slightly darkened in color, about 3 minutes. Pour in the milk, whisking until smooth, and bring to a light simmer. Remove from the heat and stir in the mustard powder. Strain the pasta and put it directly into the milk mixture. Slowly add the cheeses and stir well until melted. Add the tomatoes and jalapeños and stir. Cool the pasta down to at least room temperature before stuffing the peppers.

PREPARE THE PEPPERS: Turn your broiler to high heat and position the oven rack right below it. Lightly oil and salt the poblano peppers and place them on a sheet pan. Broil on all sides until the skin is lightly charred and blistered. Put the peppers into a large bowl, cover with plastic wrap and let sit for 15 minutes. Meanwhile, set up your breading station by putting the flour, breadcrumbs and beaten eggs into 3 separate shallow bowls. Take the poblanos out of the bowl and gently peel them. Remove the tops and scrape the insides out with a fork.

STUFF IT!: Stuff the peppers with the cooled pasta mixture. We want extra breading on the peppers to help hold them together, so we are going to do a triple layer. Start by coating the pepper in the flour and shaking the excess off. Then dip it into the egg and again let the excess drip off. Repeat these steps in the flour and the egg 2 more times. Finally, coat very well in the breadcrumbs.

COOK IT: Shallow-fry the peppers in 1 inch (2.5 cm) of vegetable oil to brown on all sides.

Sausage Tamale Stuffed Cubanelle Peppers

MAKES: 6 LARGE STUFFED PEPPERS
HEAT: 4.2
PIG-OUT SCALE: 5.1

It isn't often that I get cooking inspiration from a wedding dinner, but that exact thing happened at a wedding I went to last year. There was a chicken dish that was stuffed with a tasty polenta and studded with pine nuts and cheese. I found myself wanting to eat the polenta on its own, and I really couldn't wait to stuff something with a similar doughy corn mixture at home. I ended up doing sort of a Mexitalian spin on the idea, using a tamale dough and stuffing the whole thing into a cubanelle pepper.

FILLING

3 sausages
1 tablespoon (15 ml) olive oil
¾ cup (105 g) grits or cornmeal
3 cups (705 ml) water
1 cup (120 g) masa harina
8 ounces (225 g) pepper Jack cheese
4 ounces (112 g) chihuahua cheese
1 teaspoon black pepper
¼ cup (16 g) chopped cilantro
Salt

6 large cubanelle peppers

SAUCE

1 clove garlic
1 tablespoon (15 ml) olive oil
1 (12-ounce [336-g]) can crushed tomatoes
1 tablespoon (15 ml) chipotle-flavored Tabasco sauce
1 teaspoon cumin
2 tablespoons (30 ml) red wine vinegar

MAKE THE FILLING: Remove the sausage from the casing and brown in a frying pan with a splash of oil. Once cooked, remove from the heat and set aside, reserving the fat. In a pot, mix the grits with the water and bring to a simmer over medium heat. Cook for 2 or 3 minutes, and then remove from the heat. Add the masa harina and stir to combine. Mix in the sausages, including the fat, along with the cheeses, black pepper and cilantro. Taste and add salt if needed.

STUFF AND COOK THE PEPPERS: Preheat the oven to 325°F (170°C, or gas mark 3). Use a paring knife to cut the stems and tops off of the peppers. Use a spoon to scrape the seeds and membrane from the inside of the peppers. Stuff your filling into the peppers and be sure to really pack it in there. Bake the peppers for about 1 hour and 15 minutes.

MAKE THE SAUCE: While the peppers are in the oven, make this quick sauce. Dice the garlic and sauté it in a skillet in a little olive oil for about 3 minutes. Add all the rest of the ingredients. Bring to a quick simmer and cook for about 10 minutes. Remove from the heat. Serve the peppers with the sauce.

Pineapple Bacon Jalapeño Bites

MAKES: 40 BITES
HEAT: 6.7
PIG-OUT SCALE: 4.1

½ pineapple

10 jalapeños

4 ounces (112 g) Cheddar cheese, grated

15 slices bacon

Anyone who reads the Food in My Beard for more than 5 minutes will quickly realize that pineapple, bacon and jalapeño are one of my favorite flavor combinations. It's all right there in these three words: sweet, spicy, salty. It's great on pizza, on a burger or even in cocktails, but this recipe is the pure bare-bones expression of the combination.

• •

STUFF IT!: Cut up the pineapple into small chunks. Slice your jalapeños in half. Clean out the seeds and membrane from the jalapeños. Cut the jalapeño halves in half again the short way, so you have bite-size mini jalapeño pieces. Add a very small amount of cheese to these, followed by the pineapple. Cut your bacon slices into thirds. Take one third of the bacon and wrap it around the jalapeño. Use a toothpick to seal the bacon around the jalapeño. You should have around 40 pieces.

COOK IT: Preheat the oven to 350°F (180°C, or gas mark 4). Pop the peppers into the oven and cook until the bacon is crisp, 15 to 20 minutes.

Pork and Banana Habanero Poppers

MAKES: 15 SMALL PEPPERS
HEAT: 9.1
PIG-OUT SCALE: 4.3

15 habanero peppers
1 recipe pulled pork (page 26)
3 ripe bananas
8 ounces (225 g) cojita cheese

I decided to upgrade this popular snack to a more appropriate pepper, the habanero. They are bite-size, super flavorful and prettier than jalapeños. You just need to make sure you remove all the seeds and scrape out the ribs and membranes of the habaneros to make them bearable to eat! I stuffed these guys with pulled pork, cojita and banana, the ultimate habanero flavor complement.

PREP THE PEPPERS: Remove the tops and insides from the habaneros. Do your best to scrape out some of the white inner lining of the pepper, because this is where most of the heat lies. If you plan on touching anything for the rest of the night, you might want to use gloves.

STUFF IT!: Tuck in some pulled pork, a little slice of banana and some of the crumbled cheese. Place the peppers on a rack on a baking sheet.

COOK IT: Preheat the oven to 550˚F (285°C, or gas mark 10). Bake the peppers for about 8 minutes, until they begin to blacken.

FAIR WARNING!

When you scrape the insides out of the peppers, try not to look right into the pepper while scraping. I have done this in the past, and some of the juices from the habanero went straight into my eye! It stung for over an hour, and during that time, I could not cook or do anything but sit on my bed with my eyes closed. I thought I was going blind!

Jalapeño Popper Dog

MAKES: 4 DOGS
HEAT: 5.8
PIG-OUT SCALE: 7.2

4 thin hot dogs
12 of the biggest jalapeños you can find
6 to 8 slices American cheese
Mustard, for serving

Jalapeños seem to be monstrous at the grocery store compared to their size from a few years back. I used this large size to my advantage, and was able to case a whole hot dog and some cheese inside a couple of cut jalapeños. The fun thing about this recipe is that you could make a whole dozen of them easily, pop 'em into a zip-top bag, and head out to your nearest B.Y.O.M. party (Bring Your Own Meat), campfire, or other communal grilling situation. If you arrive at a barbecue with these you will instantly become the coolest kid at the party. This recipe is as simple as you can get, and I don't know why no one thought of it sooner!

• •

STUFF IT!: Cut the hot dogs in half the long way. Cut the top and bottom off of all of the jalapeños and remove the seeds so you have jalapeño tubes. Break the cheese so it is the same width as the hot dog, and put the pieces in between the two halves of the dog. Stuff the now cheese-stuffed hot dog into the jalapeño tubes. It should take either 2 or 3 jalapeños to cover the length of the dog.

COOK IT: Cook this low and slow to prevent too much cheese loss but also to allow the peppers to become soft and cooked, not raw and crunchy. They should be browned and heated through after about 15 minutes. Serve with some mustard!

Crab Rangoon Jalapeño Poppers

MAKES: 15 POPPERS
HEAT: 5.9
PIG-OUT SCALE: 6.7

Crab rangoon will forever be a late-night drunken snack in my mind because the Chinese restaurant by my old place was always open late. Something about that crunchy fried goodness, hot cream cheese and crab flavor really just hits the spot. Putting the filling into a jalapeño instead of a wonton really ups the drunken craving level for me. It's too bad there isn't a food truck that sells these parked in my neighborhood late at night, or maybe it's a good thing.

· ·

FILLING

8 ounces (225 g) cream cheese

5 scallions, diced, white and green parts

1 tablespoon (15 ml) soy sauce

4 ounces (112 g) imitation crab

PEPPERS

15 large jalapeño peppers

1 cup (120 g) flour

2 eggs, beaten

2 cups (230 g) panko breadcrumbs

Vegetable oil, for frying

Salt

MAKE THE FILLING: Combine all the filling ingredients in a bowl.

PREPARE THE PEPPERS: Preheat the oven to 350°F (180°C, or gas mark 4). Cut the top off the jalapeños. Use a spoon to scoop out all of the seeds and membrane from the peppers. Make a slice down one side of the peppers. Pop the peppers into the oven and let them bake for 7 to 10 minutes, until slightly softened.

STUFF IT!: Spoon the crab filling into the peppers, using the slit you made to help guide the filling all the way in. Prep your breading and frying stations, putting the flour, egg and breadcrumbs into 3 separate bowls, and setting up a drying rack for after the peppers come out of the fryer. One by one, dredge the peppers in the flour to lightly coat, then dip in the egg. We want a thick breading, so go back into the flour, followed by egg for a second time. Finally, coat with the breadcrumbs. Prep batches of 5 before frying them.

COOK IT: Preheat the oil to 350°F (180°C) in a Dutch oven. Fry the peppers in batches of 5 for about 5 minutes, until golden brown. When they come out of the fryer, season with salt immediately.

Pork and Plantain Stuffed Kale

MAKES: 5 SERVINGS
HEAT: 5.5 (WITH THE OPTIONAL HABANEROS)
PIG-OUT SCALE: 4.4

This is inspired by a Hawaiian dish called lau lau, where a piece of pork is steamed in lau lau leaves for hours until tender. Lau lau leaves aren't exactly readily available where I live, but I found that kale works to make mini versions of this. It's important to choose nice leafy kale that is firm and not at all ripped. There isn't much seasoning, so make sure you salt it liberally, and the plantain adds a nice sweetness. I like to add a little habanero when I make this, but if you don't like the heat, it still tastes great without it.

• •

2 pounds (908 g) country-style boneless pork ribs, chopped into 1½-inch (3.8-cm) cubes

Salt and pepper

3 tablespoons (45 ml) vinegar

2 habaneros, minced (optional)

2 or 3 ripe yellow plantains, peeled and sliced into ¾-inch (2-cm) rounds

2 bunches kale

Steamed rice, for serving

STUFF IT!: Liberally season the meat with salt and pepper, and then toss in the vinegar. Also add the habaneros if you are so inclined. Take one piece of meat, one plantain slice, and one kale leaf, and roll the leaf around the meat and plantain, securing it. The best method is to first cut off any stem that is too big, then wrap it as best you can, and finally seal it by poking the larger end of the stem through the softer end of the leaf.

COOK IT: Throw some kale down to line the bottom of the steamer, then add your packets of pork. Go ahead and crowd the steamer; it's no big deal. Finally, add a top layer of kale. Cover the steamer and let it steam for 2½ hours. Serve the kale and pork over some steamed rice.

Chorizo Kale and Chicken Stuffed Poblanos

MAKES: 6 TO 8 SERVINGS
HEAT: 5.3
PIG-OUT SCALE: 6.4

I've been cooking this recipe for a really long time and it never disappoints. It's fairly straightforward and is easy enough to make on a weeknight, but tastes like something much more special. Feel free to use another type of cheese if you want to tone down the heat level. Choosing the right chorizo in my opinion is the most important part of this recipe. I usually like the ground uncooked Mexican stuff, but most of the authentic Portuguese cured/smoked kind are tasty, too. Some of the more Americanized brands are a little too smoky/sweet and come off "hammy" to me.

FILLING

1 tablespoon (15 ml) olive oil

½ pound (225 g) ground chorizo

3 branches kale

8 ounces (225 g) pepper Jack cheese

8 ounces (225 g) queso blanco, crumbled

10 poblano peppers (number includes two extra in case of breakage)

4 boneless, skinless chicken breasts

MAKE THE FILLING: In a skillet over medium heat, with a little olive oil, cook the chorizo to brown it (whether it is already cooked or not). Remove the thick stems from the kale and rip the leafy parts into small pieces. Shred half the pepper Jack and combine with crumbled queso. Slice the other half of the pepper Jack into thin slices.

PREP THE POBLANOS: Broil the poblano peppers for a few minutes, turning and moving around constantly to slightly char parts of the skin and soften them up a bit. Using a paring knife, remove the stem from the peppers and shake out the seeds and insides.

PREP THE CHICKEN: Slice the chicken the long way to make 2 thin cutlets out of each breast. You may want to also pound these out to thin them further.

STUFF IT!: Top the cutlets with the chorizo, kale and cheese. Roll the cutlets up and stuff them into the poblano peppers. Try and match smaller peppers with smaller cutlets. Also, don't worry if some rip! Practice makes perfect and we can hide those rips with cheese later.

COOK IT: Preheat the oven 350°F (180°C, or gas mark 4). Bake the peppers for about 45 minutes, until fully cooked. Top with the slices of pepper Jack and broil until browned.

Goat Cheese and Orange-Basil Stuffed Cherry Peppers

MAKES: 15 TO 20 PEPPERS
HEAT: 7.1
PIG-OUT SCALE: 3.8

These little peppers combined with some of the stuffed olives on page 146 would be the perfect cocktail party apps on a summer evening. Just fill up a large platter with some sliced meats, cheeses, lots of breads and these stuffed peppers and people can just casually snack during the party. Don't tell them that cardamom is the secret ingredient, though!

. . . .

MAKE THE FILLING: Place all the filling ingredients into a food processor and process until smooth. Put the filling into a piping bag.

STUFF IT!: Sometimes the peppers are already cut and cleaned, but if the peppers are whole, remove the stems and insides with a small spoon. Pipe the filling into the peppers. Keep refrigerated until you are ready to serve.

FILLING

8 ounces (225 g) goat cheese

10 basil leaves

¼ teaspoon salt

1 tablespoon (6 g) paprika

½ teaspoon cardamom

Zest and juice of 1 orange

1 jar pickled cherry peppers (or peppadew peppers for less heat)

Stuffed Olives

Stuffing your own olives can be a little tedious, but when you are done, they can really take a charcuterie or cheese plate to the next level. Here, I have two versions—one is a simple cocktail olive with some blue cheese and pancetta, and the other is a fancy twist on a Niçoise salad.

. . . .

Blue Cheese and Pancetta Stuffed Olives

MAKES: 25 OLIVES
HEAT: 0
PIG-OUT SCALE: 3.5

MAKE THE FILLING: Pulse all the filling ingredients in a food processor until almost smooth. Fit a piping bag with a very wide tip and fill with the mixture.

STUFF IT!: Pipe the mixture into your olives. Keep refrigerated until you are ready to serve.

FILLING

5 ounces (140 g) blue cheese, crumbled

4 ounces (112 g) pancetta, cooked and crumbled

1 teaspoon chopped parsley

1 tablespoon (14 g) mayonnaise

25 of the biggest olives you can find

Tuna Niçoise Stuffed Olives

MAKES: 25 OLIVES
HEAT: 0
PIG-OUT SCALE: 3.5

FILLING

1 egg

5 green beans

6 ounces (168 g) cooked tuna

½ vine-ripened tomato, seeds and insides removed

Juice of ½ lemon

1½ teaspoons mayonnaise

½ teaspoon Dijon mustard

25 of the biggest olives you can find

PREP THE EGG AND BEANS: Place the egg in a small saucepot and cover with heavily salted, cold water. Bring to a boil. When the water comes to a full boil, drop in your green beans. After exactly 1 minute of boiling, remove the pot from the heat; 2 minutes later, remove the green beans and stop the cooking by dropping them into ice water. Allow the egg to sit in the hot water for 10 minutes total after removing from the heat. Put your egg into the ice water to stop the cooking.

MAKE THE FILLING: Flake up your tuna and chop it up really small. You want this very uniform and small so it can fit into the small olive cavity. Dice your tomato, green beans and hard-boiled egg very small as well. Add them to a bowl along with the lemon juice, mayonnaise and mustard, and mix well.

STUFF IT!: Get your olives out of the brine and ready to stuff. If you decided to torture yourself by buying olives that still have their pits, go ahead and take out the pits. Hope you have an olive pitter! Because there is only a small hole and cavity that you are going to be stuffing, you need to find a small utensil to really pack the stuffing in there. I used the end of a chopstick. Take a little bit of the tuna mixture and place it over the olive hole, and then stamp it in there like you are loading a cannon. Serve these little guys on a super fancy charcuterie plate at your next party!

ABOUT OLIVES

Traditionally, and quite obviously, this salad uses the Niçoise olive. This particular olive is a bit too small for stuffing the way we want. The best and most common variety for this recipe is the Cerignola olive, but other large olives include the Sevillano, Ascolano and Barouni varieties.

Cheddar Sriracha Stuffed Mushrooms

MAKES: 15 TO 20 MUSHROOMS
HEAT: 4.9
PIG-OUT SCALE: 4.1

Sriracha, cheese and mushrooms are not the most common flavor combination, but they actually work really well together. I first had this combo in a plate of mac and cheese and never looked back. This version takes it down to the bare bones of the three flavors, so you can taste them all come together.

• •

MAKE THE FILLING: Mix all the filling ingredients in a bowl.

STUFF IT!: Clean the mushrooms and remove the stems and ribs. Generously stuff the mushrooms with the filling. Put the mushrooms onto a baking dish.

COOK IT: Preheat the oven to 400˚F (200˚C, or gas mark 6). Roast the mushrooms for about 15 minutes. Serve hot.

FILLING

1 cup (115 g) crushed tortilla chips

1 cup (120 g) shredded Cheddar cheese

¼ cup (60 ml) Sriracha

1 shallot, minced

2 jalapeños, minced (remove seeds to tone down the heat)

15 to 20 baby bella or cremini mushrooms

Harissa Lamb Stuffed Eggplant

MAKES: 6 TO 8 SERVINGS
HEAT: 8.7
PIG-OUT SCALE: 6.4

Harissa is a red pepper paste from North Africa that is trendy right now but has been around for a very long time. Mixing it with eggplant and lamb is a natural combination, but the real fun in this recipe comes from the whipped cucumber feta topping.

. . . .

HARISSA
(or ¼ cup [44 g] store-bought)

25 dried arbol chiles

1 red bell pepper

3 cloves garlic

¼ teaspoon coriander

½ teaspoon caraway

¼ teaspoon oregano

Juice of 1 lemon

4 small (preferred) or 2 large eggplants

Olive oil

Salt and pepper

1½ pounds (680 g) ground lamb

¼ cup (16 g) chopped parsley

WHIPPED CUCUMBER FETA

8 ounces (225 g) feta

2 ounces (56 g) cream cheese

Juice of 1 lemon

1 tablespoon (15 ml) olive oil

⅓ cup (40 g) chopped cucumber

SOAK THE CHILES: Remove the stems from the chiles, and if you don't like it hot, remove the seeds too. This recipe is VERY hot, so unless you really like heat, consider removing half of the seeds to make it somewhat bearable. Even if you remove all of the seeds it will still be a solid 4 on the heat scale. Pour boiling water over the chiles to just barely cover them and allow them to sit for 20 minutes.

PREP THE EGGPLANTS: Preheat the oven to 425°F (220°C, or gas mark 7). Split the eggplants in half the long way. Generously rub with olive oil, salt and pepper. Roast the eggplants skin side down for about 30 minutes, until browned. Toss that red pepper into the oven and let it roast for the first 10 minutes with the eggplant. Remove the eggplant from the oven and turn it down to 375°F (190°C, or gas mark 5). Using a sharp spoon, make a cavern in the eggplants to put the filling, but you don't need to remove a ton. Roughly chop the removed eggplant.

MAKE THE HARISSA: Strain the chiles and add them to a food processor. Peel and seed the roasted red pepper. Add the pepper and rest of the harissa ingredients to the food processor and blend until smooth.

MAKE THE FILLING: In a hot pan with a little olive oil, sear the lamb to brown. Add the harissa paste and the eggplant insides and cook for about 5 to 7 minutes, until well combined. Remove from the heat and stir in parsley.

STUFF AND COOK: Spoon the lamb mixture into the eggplants, leaving any excess fat behind. Place on a baking sheet and roast the eggplants for 30 minutes.

MAKE THE WHIPPED FETA: Add the feta and cream cheese to the bowl of a food processor and pulse until smooth. Add the rest of the ingredients and let it whip for 1 minute. Taste and add salt if needed. Serve the feta on the side with the eggplants.

Chicken Curry Stuffed Portobellos

MAKES: 4 OR 5 MUSHROOMS
HEAT: 3.5
PIG-OUT SCALE: 2.5

This recipe always brings back pleasant memories of grilling on the beach in Bermuda. My friend Felicia would bring these curry stuffed portobellos to the party, which, as it turns out, work perfectly on a bun instead of a burger. Don't let the word *curry* intimidate you, though; this recipe is very easy. If you aren't heading to a beach BBQ, they also work over rice.

. . . .

MARINADE

1 cup (225 g) plain yogurt

½ teaspoon salt

1 heaping teaspoon curry powder (ideally homemade, page 191)

5 cloves garlic

2-inch (5-cm) piece ginger

2 pounds (908 g) boneless, skinless chicken thighs

2 large onions

1 tablespoon (14 g) butter

Salt

4 or 5 portobello mushrooms

MARINATE THE CHICKEN: Mix the yogurt with the salt and curry powder. Grate in the garlic and ginger with a microplane grater. Add the chicken, turn to coat in the marinade, cover with plastic wrap and let it sit in the fridge for at least an hour, if not overnight.

COOK THE CHICKEN: Roughly dice the onion. Melt the butter in a large frying pan or Dutch oven. Cook the onion over medium heat until deeply browned, stirring often, about 15 minutes. Season with salt as needed. Add the chicken and continue to cook over medium heat, stirring occasionally, until the chicken is tender and shredding, about 35-40 minutes. Break up the chicken into small shreds by just mashing it up with your utensil.

PREP THE MUSHROOMS: Clean and trim the mushrooms, removing the stem and all the ribs under the cap.

STUFF AND COOK: If you are making this recipe in your house, heat up a cast-iron grill pan, or just any frying pan, and cook the mushrooms open side down for about 5 minutes. Remove them from the heat, stuff them with the filling and then cook them another 7 or so minutes, open side up, covered, until the mushrooms are tender and the chicken is heated through.

If you are taking these to go, intending to grill them at a barbecue or tailgate situation, stuff the caps and get them in the fridge until it's time to go. You can put them into individual zip-top bags, or use a gallon-size bag with some parchment paper to keep them separated. Cook the mushrooms over super low heat for about 12 minutes, making sure they are covered well so they cook through before burning.

Pasta Salad Stuffed Tomatoes

MAKES: 20 TOMATOES
HEAT: 2.2
PIG-OUT SCALE: 3.9

This pasta salad was my mom's specialty for many years, but after I got the recipe from her I wasn't quite as keen on it. I mean, don't get me wrong, it was still delicious, but it was 90 percent packaged and bottled items and loaded with things like sodium and corn syrup that I try to avoid when I can. I re-created the pasta salad but with fresh ingredients and it came out even better! Stuffing it into these tomatoes is a fun way to serve it at a barbecue. It tastes good cold, baked for a few minutes or even tossed onto the grill.

20 vine-ripened tomatoes

DRESSING

¼ cup (60 ml) olive oil
½ cup (120 ml) red wine vinegar
1 teaspoon paprika
1 tablespoon (4 g) chopped fresh oregano
½ cup (50 g) grated Pecorino Romano
3 ounces (84 g) sliced pepperoni
1 teaspoon celery seed
1 teaspoon sesame seed

1 pound (454 g) spaghetti
Feta cheese, for garnish

PREPARE THE TOMATOES: For each tomato, slice off the very top, then core out all of the insides, creating a nice tomato bowl. Reserve the insides and tops of the tomatoes. Get rid of the seeds, but dice everything else and put into a large bowl.

MAKE THE DRESSING: In that same bowl, add the oil, vinegar, paprika, chopped oregano and cheese. Dice the pepperoni and add that. In a spice grinder, coffee grinder or mortar and pestle, roughly grind the celery seed and sesame seed. Add to the bowl.

COOK THE PASTA: Bring a pot of salted water to a boil over high heat. Break the spaghetti in half and drop it into the water. Cook the pasta according to package directions until al dente and strain. Put the pasta right into the dressing and mix well. Allow to cool.

STUFF IT!: Line up your tomatoes. Using a fork, twirl some spaghetti as if you were going to take a huge bite. Stick the fork into the tomato with all the pasta on it, then, using your hand to help, remove the fork from the tomato, leaving the pasta inside. Top with a few crumbles of feta.

SERVE: These tomatoes are great cold, but they are also great hot. You can toss them onto the grill for 5 minutes just to warm them a little and char up the tomato, or broil them for a minute to brown the cheese.

Bacon Avocado Chicken Salad Stuffed Tomatoes

MAKES: 20 TOMATOES
HEAT: 2.9
PIG-OUT SCALE: 3.3

20 vine-ripened tomatoes

FILLING

10 slices bacon

2 boneless, skinless chicken breasts (about ½ pound [225 g] total)

1½ teaspoons salt, plus more for sprinkling on chicken

1 tablespoon (15 ml) oil

3 cloves garlic

1 onion

1 jalapeño

1 bunch cilantro

Juice of 2 limes

5 avocados

This fresh chicken salad is basically guac with chicken in it. It was always something I made while trying to healthify chicken salad by replacing the mayo. For this version, however, I de-healthified it by adding some bacon, but it tastes so good that it's worth it.

PREPARE THE TOMATOES: For each tomato, slice off the very top of the tomato, then core out all of the insides, creating a nice tomato bowl. Reserve the insides and tops of the tomatoes. Get rid of the seeds and wet stuff around the seeds, but dice everything else and put into a large bowl.

MAKE THE FILLING: Cut the bacon slices into half. Cook on medium to render fat. Cool until crispy, about 10 minutes. Remove and set aside. Drain about half the fat. Sprinkle the chicken with salt and cook in a frying pan with the remaining bacon fat until lightly browned and cooked through, about 20 minutes. Remove from the pan and chop and shred the chicken. Put it into the fridge to cool. Grate the garlic with a microplane into the bowl with the tomatoes. Dice the onion and jalapeño very small and add them to the bowl. Chop up the cilantro and add to the bowl. Add the 1½ teaspoons salt and the lime juice. Finally, peel and seed the avocados and add them to the bowl with everything else. Mash up the avocados with all the rest of the ingredients. Add the cooled shredded chicken and mix.

STUFF IT!: Line up your tomatoes. Using a spoon, scoop as much guac as will fit into each tomato. Chill the tomatoes for about 30 minutes. Sprinkle the tomatoes with the bacon just before serving. If you want to make these ahead of time, because of the amount of lime juice, they should be fine in the fridge without browning for about 2 hours, loosely covered. If you want to wait longer, it would be best to keep the guac mixture in a large bowl with plastic wrap protecting it, and then stuff it into the tomatoes when it's closer to serving time. Top each tomato with one of the bacon slices before serving.

Thai Coconut Chicken Stuffed Cabbage

MAKES: 12 TO 15 ROLLS
HEAT: 6.5
PIG-OUT SCALE: 2.3

Where I grew up, there is a large Polish community, and stuffed cabbage, or galumpkis, is a common dish. I always liked galumpkis, but I wanted to put a fun and different spin on it. For this version, I replaced the sweet and sour tomato sauce with a sweet and sour Thai coconut broth. On the inside of the cabbage are things commonly served in that broth, like chicken, snap peas and mushrooms. Every bite is like eating a bowl of tom kha kai (chicken galangal soup)!

SAUCE

5 lemongrass stalks

2 (14-ounce [400-ml]) cans coconut milk

2 cups (470 ml) chicken stock

20 kaffir lime leaves

Stalks and roots of 1 bunch cilantro

2 chunks fresh or dried galangal (if you can find it)

2 teaspoons fish sauce

1 tablespoon (6 g) lime zest

FILLING

1½ pounds (680 g) ground chicken

1½ cups (105 g) chopped mushrooms

1 cup (75 g) chopped snap peas

5 to 10 Thai red chiles, minced

3 cloves garlic, minced

1-inch (2.5-cm) piece ginger, minced

½ bunch cilantro, chopped

1 cup (70 g) cooked rice noodles

1 tablespoon (15 ml) fish sauce

½ teaspoon salt

1 head green cabbage

1 or 2 limes, cut into wedges

STEEP THE SAUCE: Bruise and break the lemongrass with the back of your knife. Combine all of the sauce ingredients in a heavy-bottomed pot and bring to a simmer over medium heat. Cook for 30 to 45 minutes. Strain into a bowl.

MAKE THE FILLING: Combine all of the filling ingredients in a bowl.

STUFF IT!: Bring a large pot of salted water to a boil. Prepare the cabbage by removing some of the outer damaged leaves. Carefully remove 12 to 15 large leaves without damaging them. Blanch the cabbage leaves for 5 to 7 minutes, until they are soft enough to wrap. Divide the chicken mixture into 12 to 15 equal parts. Stuff the cabbage with the chicken mixture and wrap tightly.

COOK IT: Preheat the oven to 350°F (180°C, or gas mark 4). Put a ladle of the sauce on the bottom of the baking dish. Line up the cabbage rolls with the seam side down and ladle more sauce over the top until it comes about three-fourths of the way up the cabbage. You probably won't use it all. Bake for 1 hour, or until the meat is cooked through.

Allow to cool for 5 minutes before serving. Serve with the lime wedges, and don't forget because the lime juice is essential to the flavor of the dish.

Meat Stuffed Twice Baked Potatoes

MAKES: 12 POTATO HALVES
HEAT: 0
PIG-OUT SCALE: 7.2

6 large baking potatoes
Olive oil
Salt

FILLING

½ pound (225 g) ground beef

½ pound (225 g) sausage

2 tablespoons (28 g) butter

1 onion, diced

1 celery stalk, diced

2 cloves garlic, minced

¼ cup (16 g) chopped parsley

½ cup (60 g) breadcrumbs

½ cup (120 ml) chicken stock, or as needed

The stuffing in these potatoes is actually something that my grandmother used to make every Thanksgiving, called meat stuffing. I thought that the meat stuffing would be tasty right in a twice-baked potato. The potato ends up catching all the juice while the stuffing cooks and developing a really nice flavor.

• •

BAKE THE POTATOES: Preheat the oven to 350°F (180°C, or gas mark 4).

Scrub and wash the potatoes. Poke with a fork a few times to allow the steam to escape and help them cook faster. Lightly rub with some olive oil and sprinkle with salt and lay on a baking sheet. Bake until the potatoes are tender, about 1 hour. Remove from the oven and let cool. Increase the oven temperature to 400°F (200°C, or gas mark 6).

MAKE THE FILLING: While the potatoes bake, cook the beef and sausage together to brown. Remove from the pan and drain off the fat. In the same pan, add the butter and sauté the onion and celery with a pinch of salt. When they have sweated for about 7 minutes, add the garlic. Transfer to a large bowl and add the parsley, breadcrumbs and just enough chicken stock to moisten everything.

STUFF IT!: Cut the baked potatoes in half and then scoop the insides leaving the skin and some potato to use as a bowl. Mash the potato insides and add to the meat mixture. Taste and add salt if needed. Scoop the meat filling into the potatoes, really loading it in.

BAKE AGAIN: Return the potatoes to the oven and bake for 30 minutes longer.

Lamb Vindaloo Stuffed Onions

Someone brought stuffed onions to a Thanksgiving party I was having and I was stunned by the idea. I had just never seen it or even thought about it, and my brain was spinning about what would truly be the best thing to put into these babies. I finally settled on lamb vindaloo. You may not realize it, but vindaloo is a very onion-based dish, and roasting it in an onion only enhances the flavors.

· ·

MAKES: 4 TO 6 SERVINGS
HEAT: 7.0
PIG-OUT SCALE: 5.1

10 medium-large onions

VINDALOO PASTE

2 tablespoons (28 g) butter
Salt
7 cloves garlic, smashed
1-inch (2.5-cm) piece ginger, sliced against the grain to cut down the stringiness
2 heaping tablespoons (12 g) curry powder, homemade (page 191) or store-bought
2 teaspoons coriander
10 Thai chiles, diced

FILLING

2 pounds (908 g) lamb shoulder
Salt
1 tablespoon (15 ml) vegetable oil
¼ cup (60 ml) vinegar
Pinch of brown sugar

1 cup (235 ml) water, for the pan
Basmati rice, for serving

PREP THE ONIONS: Cut about 1 inch (2.5 cm) off the top of each onion so that there is a 2-inch (5-cm) circle. Cut just a hair off of the bottom of the onion so it will sit flat. Peel any paper layers off of the onion. Use a sharp spoon or melon baller to cut the insides of the onion out. Depending on how thick the onion layers are, you want one or two layers intact to act as the vessel. Set the onion cups aside and save the onion insides.

MAKE THE PASTE: Roughly chop the reserved onion insides and get them into a medium-hot pan with the butter. Lightly season with salt and cook for 15 to 20 minutes, until the onions reach a deep brown color all the way through. Add the garlic, ginger, curry powder, coriander and chiles and cook for about 2 minutes, stirring often. Put the onion mixture into a food processor and blend until smooth.

MAKE THE FILLING: Dice the lamb into 1-inch (2.5-cm) cubes and remove any visible fat. Season the meat with salt. In a hot pan with a splash of vegetable oil, sear the pieces of lamb to brown on all sides. Add the vinegar and sugar, followed by the curry paste and stir to combine. Simmer the vindaloo for about 20 minutes, until the lamb is cooked through. Remove from the heat.

STUFF IT!: Divide the lamb chunks among the onion cups. Line the onions in a baking dish. Pour any additional curry from the pan into the onions, and then into the bottom of the pan if the onions are full. Add the water to the bottom of the pan and cover with a sheet of foil.

COOK IT: Preheat the oven to 350°F (180°C, or gas mark 4). Bake for 30 minutes. Remove the cover and bake for 30 minutes more, until the lamb is tender and the onions have lightly browned. Serve the onions over basmati rice.

Fish and Chip Tots

Do you love fish and chips but hate the extra effort of having to eat the fish separately from the chips??? (Cue black-and-white video of people having trouble eating fish and chips.) Well, you are in luck! I had the idea for these tots after eating a classic Italian bacalao (salt cod) preparation. The salt cod was soaked to remove some of the saltiness and then mixed with potato and deep-fried. I thought, why not skip out on the whole salting then un-salting process and just try it with fresh cod? They came out really great. Dipped in a makeshift tartar sauce, these tots are pub food perfection.

SPICY NOT-TARTAR SAUCE

1½ cups (340 g) mayonnaise

1 pickle

¼ cup (60 ml) Sriracha

TOTS

3 medium Yukon gold potatoes

Salt and pepper

Vegetable oil, for coating potatoes and frying

1 egg

2 teaspoons thyme

2 to 4 tablespoons (16 to 32 g) flour, plus more for dusting

1¼ pounds (568 g) cod fish

MAKE THE SAUCE: Put the sauce ingredients into a food processor and blend until it's fairly smooth.

MAKE THE TOTS: Preheat the oven to 350°F (176°C, or gas mark 4). Season the potatoes with salt and pepper and lightly coat in oil. Roast until tender, but just slightly undercooked, a little over 1 hour.

Roughly chop the potatoes, and mix them in a bowl with the egg, thyme, flour and salt and pepper to taste. Use more or less flour as needed to help the potatoes form a nice starchy mixture. Allow the potatoes to mostly mash, but retain some chunks.

STUFF IT!: Spread some flour on a large plate. Chop the fish into about ¾-inch (2-cm) chunks. One by one with the chunks of fish, grab enough potato mixture to wrap around the fish and seal it inside. Don't overdo it with the potato; you want a nice ratio. Put the ball of potato onto the plate of flour. Form the potato into the internationally recognized tater-tot shape. Continue until all of the tots are made.

FRY: Bring the vegetable oil to 350°F (180°C, or gas mark 4) in a heavy-bottomed pot or Dutch oven. Fry the fish tots for about 5 minutes each until nicely browned and the fish is cooked through. Serve with the dipping sauce.

Spicy Pineapple Roll

MAKES: 3 AS AN APPETIZER
HEAT: 4.3
PIG-OUT SCALE: 1.3

While removing the core from a fresh pineapple one day, I made the realization that the inside of the pineapple could nicely house some sort of stuffing. Taking inspiration from a sushi roll, I decided that rice would be a perfect filling. The result was an inverted roll where pineapple was the wrapper, with rice and jalapeño as the filling. Serve this on a bed of crispy tempura bits with a dab of Sriracha sauce and you have a bite of food that hits all the right flavor and textural notes.

RICE

½ cup (80 g) sushi rice
½ cup (120 ml) water
1½ teaspoons sugar
1½ teaspoons rice vinegar
1 teaspoon salt

TEMPURA BATTER

½ cup (120 ml) soda water
⅔ cup (66 g) flour
½ tablespoon corn starch
Vegetable oil, for frying
5 ice cubes

1 ripe pineapple
4 large jalapeños
Sriracha sauce, for serving

MAKE THE RICE: Rinse the rice and place in a pot with the water. Heat on high to bring to a simmer. Turn the heat to low, cover and let cook for 10 to 15 minutes, until the rice is tender. Remove from the heat and let stand another 10 minutes. Transfer to a large bowl, add the sugar, vinegar and salt, and mix with a paddle to cool and combine. When cooled after about 10 minutes of mixing, it should be sticky and have the texture and taste you have come to expect from sushi rice.

MAKE THE TEMPURA: Whisk together all the tempura ingredients in a large bowl (including the ice cubes). Bring ½ inch (1.3 cm) of oil to 350°F (180°C) in a frying pan. Drizzle the tempura batter into the oil (avoiding the ice) and fry for a minute or two until crispy and very lightly browned.

STUFF IT!: Remove the core from the pineapple (see sidebar). To prep the jalapeños, remove the stem and tip first. Next, peel the jalapeños carefully with a paring knife. Finally, remove the seeds and insides from the jalapeños. Drop the first jalapeño into the hole in the pineapple. Add sushi rice and stuff it right in there to seal all the gaps. Continue with the next jalapeño and more rice until the entire shaft is filled. Finally, pare down the pineapple by whittling away at the outer parts until you have a nice compact roll. You could really do this in any shape you want, but I found a circle to be the most aesthetic for my tastes.

Arrange the tempura flakes on a plate. Slice your pineapple roll into bite-size pieces, and lay them down on the plate. Garnish with a small squirt of Sriracha on each roll.

JOURNEY TO THE CENTER OF THE PINEAPPLE

Keeping the pineapple body intact is the key to this recipe. A long and skinny knife would do the trick, but be very careful to keep a tight circle cut. Try a small cookie cutter, or dig the core out with a grapefruit spoon. If you cut the pineapple in half, the tunnel will become a little more manageable, and it won't affect the end product.

Chana Masala Stuffed Grape Leaves

Persian grape leaves are a tasty treat that I often throw into my order when I get Persian takeout, but I had never made them until very recently. My version uses an Indian chickpea curry as the filling instead of lentils and rice. They are super flavorful and have a nice kick!

• •

MAKES: 30 GRAPE LEAVES
HEAT: 5.8
PIG-OUT SCALE: 3.9

FILLING

1 tablespoon (15 ml) olive oil

1 onion, diced

1½ teaspoons grated garlic

1½ teaspoons grated ginger

6 Thai red chiles, diced

1 tablespoon (6 g) curry powder, homemade (page 191) or store-bought

1 teaspoon turmeric

1 teaspoon mustard powder

1 (14-ounce [392-g]) can petite diced tomatoes

1½ cups (360 g) cooked chickpeas

1½ cups (250 g) cooked rice

30 jarred grape leaves, plus about 4 to line the pot

1 cup (235 ml) water

⅓ cup (80 ml) lime juice

1 tablespoon (12 g) sugar

MAKE THE FILLING: In a hot pan with a splash of oil, cook the onion until lightly browned, about 20 minutes. Add the garlic, ginger, chiles and spices and stir well, cooking for about 2 minutes. Add the tomatoes, chickpeas and rice and stir to combine. If it appears too liquidy, simmer for 10 minutes to cook off some of the juices.

STUFF IT!: Rinse the grape leaves really well. One by one, roll up about 2 tablespoons (30 g) of filling into each grape leaf. Line a heavy-bottomed pot with the extra grape leaves. Add the rolled grape leaves on top.

COOK IT: Mix the water with the lime juice and sugar and pour it over the grape leaves. Cook over medium-low heat for about 30 minutes. Serve as a side, snack, or app.

Bacon Stuffed Peaches

MAKES: 8 PEACH HALVES
HEAT: 0
PIG-OUT SCALE: 7.2

FILLING

8 strips bacon, cooked
1 packed cup (20 g) arugula
8 ounces (225 g) mascarpone cheese
2 tablespoons black pepper

4 peaches
Olive oil
Salt

It doesn't get any better than recipes like this one in the summertime. Serve this simple side with a nice steak or hunk of barbecued chicken and you don't need anything else (except maybe a beer or some sangria).

MAKE THE FILLING: Pulse the bacon, arugula, cheese and pepper in a food processor with a little salt. Keep it somewhat chunky.

GRILL AND STUFF: Split the peaches in half and remove the pits. Brush the peaches with olive oil and light salt. Then grill open side down for about 5 minutes to get some nice grill marks. Remove from the grill and stuff the peaches with the bacon mixture. Return to the grill and cook for another 5 minutes with the grill closed.

Pork Stuffed Apple Rings

This strange idea popped into my head after I made the pineapple roll. Basically, I thought to myself, "Hmmm . . . what else can I do this to?" This is sort of the beginning of the idea, but you could take it many different places. Bake these lying on their side with some sort of sauce and you have apple cannelloni or manicotti. Serve them whole with rice, or cut them up into bite-size appetizers with some dipping sauce. Any way you do it, it's a unique concept with creative flavors and textures that are sure to wow your guests.

Juice of 1 lemon
8 apples

FILLING
½ pound (225 g) ground pork
¼ cup (25 g) grated Parmesan cheese
1 clove garlic, grated
1 egg
¼ cup (30 g) breadcrumbs
4 scallions, diced
1 teaspoon salt

PREPARE THE APPLES: Fill a bowl with water and squeeze the lemon into it. You will dip your prepped apples in here to keep them from turning brown. The key to this recipe is having the rings that help you slice the apples into tubes. The right size cookie cutters will do it, but I have these nice round metal tubes of varying diameters that I use for situations like this. You need to first cut out the core, then use a slightly larger cutter to make the apple into a tube. You could also use just a plain apple corer and then whittle away the apple to get the desired tube shape.

MAKE THE FILLING: Combine the filling ingredients in a large bowl.

STUFF AND BAKE: Preheat the oven to 350°F (180°C, or gas mark 4).

Use a chopstick to stuff the filling into the apples like you are loading a cannon. Line up the apples in a baking dish and bake for about 45 minutes.

These can then be sliced like a maki roll and eaten as appetizers, or served like cannelloni over some rice or pasta. Another fun way to serve them would be to first slice them into rounds, then pan-fry them in a little butter to brown up on both sides.

iv. Ginger root

v. Cinnamon

ii. Granola

i. Pie Crust

iii. Apples

CHAPTER 5:

StuffeD Sweets

I like my desserts to be over-the-top, so you can imagine how fun it was for me to come up with a handful of stuffed sweets. How over-the-top you ask? There is a whole cherry pie stuffed into a chocolate cake. Is that enough for you? Well, what about an 11-inch (28-cm) peanut butter cup? Looking for some heat? Try the candied habanero pizzelles that are so delicious you won't care that your tongue is burning off!

Cherry Pie Stuffed Chocolate Cake

One day I baked a pie, then I made some cake batter, and just dropped that pie into the middle and baked it. It's kind of a ridiculous scenario when you think about it, but when you cut into that chocolate cake and the cherry pie filling oozes out of the center, it's all worth it.

MAKES: 15 SERVINGS
HEAT: 0
PIG-OUT SCALE: 9.6

CHERRY PIE

6 cups (930 g) pitted cherries
¾ cup (150 g) granulated sugar
2 teaspoons vanilla extract
Pinch of salt
¼ cup (30 g) cornstarch
1 box refrigerated pie crust

CHOCOLATE CAKE

4 cups (480 g) flour
2 cups (400 g) granulated sugar
¾ cup (90 g) cocoa powder
2 teaspoons baking soda
1 teaspoon baking powder
1 teaspoon salt
2 large eggs
1 cup (235 ml) milk
½ cup (120 ml) vegetable oil
2 teaspoons vanilla extract
1 cup (235 ml) hot coffee (I usually use good-quality instant)

· ·

NOTES ABOUT EQUIPMENT: This amount of filling works great with a 9-inch (23-cm) pie dish, but if you have a smaller pie dish you should use that instead. The 9-inch (23-cm) pie is really unruly to work with, and you need an extra-large cake pan later when you are baking the pie inside the cake. I did this once with this exact recipe in a 9-inch (23-cm) pie dish, then I baked the cake in a parchment-lined Dutch oven.

If you happen to have a rare 5½-inch (14-cm) pie pan, I would suggest using that and then using a normal size 9-inch (23-cm) cake pan (as long as it has higher edges). If you do this, you can reduce the recipe by one-third.

MAKE THE PIE: Preheat the oven to 425°F (220°C, or gas mark 7). Mix together the cherries, granulated sugar, vanilla, salt and cornstarch. Line your pie tin with one of the pie crusts. Fill with the cherry filling, and top with the other pie crust. Make a few slits in the top crust to allow the steam to escape, and be sure to cut any excess crust off and seal the edges.

Put the pie into the oven with a pan underneath in case any of the filling boils over. Bake for 10 minutes, then turn the oven down to 375°F (190°C, or gas mark 5) and bake for another 40 minutes, until everything is browned and bubbly. Remove from the oven and let the pie cool completely in the fridge for about 2 hours.

MAKE THE CAKE BATTER: Grease and line your cake pan (see above for pan sizes). Mix the flour, granulated sugar, cocoa powder, baking soda, baking powder and salt in a large bowl. In another bowl, add the eggs, milk, oil and vanilla and beat until combined. Pour the wet ingredients into the dry and mix until well combined. Pour the hot coffee over the batter and mix well.

(continued)

Cherry Pie StuffeD Chocolate Cake (cont.)

FROSTING

3 cups (360 g) confectioner's sugar

¾ cup (90 g) unsweetened cocoa

½ cup (112 g) butter, softened

¼ cup (60 ml) heavy cream

1 teaspoon vanilla extract

STUFF IT!: Pour the batter into the cake pan, reserving about 1 cup (235 ml). Being really careful, flip your pie upside down onto a flat cookie sheet or cutting board. Slide the pie off of the board and into the cake batter. If it doesn't quite sink enough, gently push it down, and then pour the remaining cake batter on top to cover any exposed pie.

COOK IT: Preheat the oven to 350°F (180°C, or gas mark 4). Bake the cake for almost 1 hour, but start checking in on it at about 40 minutes, using a wooden skewer to test for doneness. When it is done, allow it to cool in the pan for about 20 minutes, then flip it and let it cool for at least an hour before frosting.

MAKE THE FROSTING: Put all the frosting ingredients in a large bowl and beat until smooth. Frost the cake after it has cooled.

Basil Cheesecake Stuffed Strawberries

MAKES: 22 STUFFED STRAWBERRIES
HEAT: 0
PIG-OUT SCALE: 7.9

22 strawberries (about 1 ¼ pounds [568 g])

8 ounces (225 g) cream cheese

1 (7 ½-ounce [210 g]) container Marshmallow Fluff

15 basil leaves

Strawberry and basil are a favorite flavor combination of mine, whether it be sweet or savory. This is a shortcut cheesecake recipe that doesn't need baking and is perfect for stuffing into ripe strawberries on a hot summer afternoon.

• •

Use a melon baller to remove the tops and hollow out the strawberries. Mix together the cream cheese and fluff, ideally in a stand mixer, but you can do it without. Chiffonade the basil and stir it in. Fill a piping bag with the fluff mixture and, using a decorative tip, pipe the mixture into the strawberries.

Ginger-Cinnamon Baked Apples

These baked apples aren't the most craved or requested dessert around, but on a nice crisp fall day they really hit the spot. Also, they are fairly healthy for a dessert, so they can come in handy to satisfy a sweet tooth during a diet.

Juice of 1 lemon

6 apples

¼ cup (50 g) granulated sugar, plus more for sprinkling

1 cup (225 g) granola

1 tablespoon (7 g) grated ginger

¼ cup (60 g) packed brown sugar

1 teaspoon vanilla extract

1 teaspoon cinnamon

½ teaspoon plus a pinch salt

1 refrigerated pie crust

1 egg, beaten, mixed with ¼ cup (60 ml) water

1 cup (235 ml) water

Vanilla ice cream, for serving

PREPARE THE APPLES: Fill a bowl with water and mix in the lemon juice. This will keep your apples from browning. Core the apples, removing the tops and insides and leaving a nice cavity for the filling. Dip your prepared apples into the lemon water before lining them up in a baking dish. Reserve the insides of the apples and dice what is usable (not core or seed) until you have 1 cup (150 g). Lightly dust the apples with the granulated sugar, allowing some to get in the bottom of the pan.

STUFF IT!: In a large bowl, combine the granola, ginger, brown sugar, vanilla, cinnamon and the pinch of salt with the cup of diced apple. Fill your apples with the mixture, packing it in.

Roll out the pie crust and cut into 6 rounds, approximately 3 inches (7.5 cm) in diameter. Top each apple with one pie crust round. Lightly brush the pie crusts with the egg wash. Sprinkle some additional sugar on top. Microwave the water with the remaining ½ teaspoon salt for 1½ minutes. Pour the salted water into the bottom of the pan with the apples.

COOK IT!: Preheat the oven to 350°F (180°C, or gas mark 4). Bake the apples for about 1 hour, until the crust is nicely browned, the apples are fork tender, and the water on the bottom of the pan has turned into a syrup. Serve the apples with a little bit of the syrup from the pan and a nice big scoop of vanilla ice cream.

Piña Colada Stuffed Panna Cotta

MAKES: 6 PANNA COTTA
HEAT: 0
PIG-OUT SCALE: 5.8

PINEAPPLE PURÉE

1 cup (165 g) pineapple chunks

1 tablespoon (13 g) sugar

PANNA COTTA

20 cardamom pods

1 cup (235 ml) cream

1 (14-ounce [400-ml]) can coconut milk

½ cup (100 g) sugar

3 tablespoons (45 ml) water

2½ teaspoons gelatin

Coconut flakes

Freezing the pineapple purée allows it to hide in the center of the panna cotta, and while the gelatin sets up, the pineapple unfreezes. In the end, this leaves us with an effect almost like a lava cake, where the pineapple comes oozing out when the panna cotta is cut.

. . . .

NOTES ABOUT EQUIPMENT: You'll need a smaller ice cube tray. This could be a novelty shape, just circles or a mini cube tray made for college kids, but it has to be only about 1 tablespoon (15 ml) in size.

PREP THE RAMEKINS: Butter the ramekins and dust with sugar, tapping out any excess.

MAKE THE PINEAPPLE PURÉE: Purée the pineapple and the sugar in a food processor until smooth. Pour the pineapple into the ice cube tray and freeze.

MAKE THE PANNA COTTA: Crack open the cardamom pods and gather the seeds, discarding the husks. Heat the cream, coconut milk, sugar and cardamom seeds in a pot until simmering. Allow to cook for about 5 minutes, stirring often. Meanwhile, mix the water and gelatin in a large bowl. Pour the cream mixture through a strainer over the water and gelatin. Stir to combine well. Pour into the ramekins and refrigerate for 1 hour.

STUFF IT!: After the first hour when the panna cotta has slightly set up, tuck an ice cube into each one. Refrigerate for another 6 hours. It will be set up after another hour, but the fruit purée will not have thawed yet.

TOAST THE COCONUT: Preheat the oven to 350°F (180°C, or gas mark 4). Spread the coconut out onto a baking sheet and toast for about 15 minutes, until browned. Stir if needed during cooking.

SERVE: To unmold the panna cotta, run a knife around the edges and flip onto a plate. Top with the toasted coconut flakes and serve.

Avocado Éclairs

I could drink pastry cream with a straw, and this avocado version is no different. Well, let me rephrase that. It's no different because I would also drink it with a straw, but it is VERY different than normal pastry cream. It is loaded with sweet and tart lime flavors, and of course, that unique avocado green. The only downside is that you can't make this too far ahead of time or the filling will turn brown.

. . . .

DOUGH

½ cup (112 g) unsalted butter
1 cup (235 ml) water
¼ teaspoon salt
1 cup (120 g) flour
4 large eggs

FILLING

1 vanilla bean
2 cups (470 ml) whole milk
6 egg yolks
¾ cup (150 g) sugar
¼ cup (30 g) cornstarch
2 avocados, pitted and peeled
¼ cup (60 ml) lime juice
1 teaspoon lime zest

GANACHE

½ cup (120 ml) cream
6 ounces (168 g) bittersweet chocolate

MAKE THE DOUGH: Preheat the oven to 450°F (230°C, or gas mark 8). In a pot, bring the butter, water and salt to a boil over high heat. Remove from the heat and vigorously mix in the flour. Return to the heat and continue mixing, about 30 seconds, being careful not to let any dough get stuck to the bottom of the pan or burn.

Put the dough into a stand mixer with the paddle attachment, turn on medium speed, and add the eggs one at a time. Only add the next egg when the previous one is fully incorporated.

Put the dough into a pastry bag. Line a baking sheet with parchment paper. Pipe the dough onto the baking sheet in strips about 4 to 5 inches (10 to 12.5 cm) long and nice and fat. This should make about 8. Bake for about 10 minutes, then reduce the heat to 350°F (180°C, or gas mark 4) and bake for 20 more minutes, until they are lightly browned and feel hollow when tapped.

MAKE THE FILLING: Split the vanilla bean and scrape out the seeds. Put the milk into a small saucepan with the vanilla bean and seeds and stir to combine. Bring to a simmer but watch it because it will easily boil over. Once it starts boiling, immediately remove from the heat and let it sit for about 10 minutes. Meanwhile, whisk the egg yolks with the sugar until lightened in color. Add the cornstarch and continue whisking. Whisk in half of the milk mixture until combined, then add it all back to the original saucepan with the milk. Heat this mixture to a quick boil, then remove from the heat. Allow to cool in the fridge with a sheet of plastic wrap covering it to prevent a skin from forming. This can be made up to a day in advance.

STUFF IT!: When it's time to go, put the avocado, lime juice and lime zest, into the food processor and blend until smooth. Grab your pastry cream and fold the avocado mixture in. Put it all into a pastry bag and pipe it into the éclairs, making sure it is nice and full, but not exploding out of the pastry.

MAKE THE GANACHE: Microwave the cream in a bowl for 1½ minutes. Pour the cream over the chocolate in another bowl and stir until the chocolate is fully melted and the mixture is smooth. If this doesn't happen within about 2 minutes, microwave the mixture for 30 seconds and keep trying. Pour the chocolate into a shallow bowl and one by one dip the top of the éclairs into the chocolate. Allow to cool in the refrigerator and serve cold. These should not sit more than 6 hours or the avocado will begin to brown.

Stuffed Cookies

MAKES: 12 TO 24 COOKIES DEPENDING ON THE STUFFING
HEAT: 0
PIG-OUT SCALE: 8.7

It occurred to me that cookie dough is very moldable, and anything moldable is therefore stuffable. The fun thing about this recipe is that anything is fair game to put in these cookies. I have compiled a list of things that I think would work well, but half the fun is trying new things yourself. Even the failures come out delicious!

• •

COOKIES

1 cup (225 g) butter, softened
¾ cup (170 g) packed brown sugar
¾ cup (150 g) granulated sugar
2 eggs
1 tablespoon (15 ml) vanilla extract
3 cups (360 g) flour
1 teaspoon baking soda
1 teaspoon salt

FILLING IDEAS

Puffed rice cereal
Peanut butter cups
Oreos
Various Girl Scout cookies
Nutter Butter cookies
A whole s'more
A brownie
Pizza bagels
Car keys (kidding!)

MAKE THE COOKIES: In a stand mixer, cream the butter and both sugars until lightened in color. Add the eggs and vanilla and mix until combined. Meanwhile, combine the flour, baking soda and salt in a large bowl. Slowly add the dry ingredients to the mixer, pretty much in thirds, until it is all incorporated. Shut off the mixer and get the dough into the fridge while you get everything ready for stuffing.

PREPARE THE FILLING: Prepare whatever you need for the filling.

STUFF IT!: Stuffing the cookies is as easy as getting the cookie dough around the filling you are stuffing. You could add chocolate chips to the dough if you want, but I usually don't to make it easier. Wrap the dough around the filling, being very thorough and sealing it up well, but also don't load on the dough. Make sure there is a little more dough on top of the filling than on the bottom because it will settle downward when it starts to bake. Place the cookies on a baking sheet.

BAKE IT: Preheat the oven to 350°F (180°C, or gas mark 4). Bake the cookies for about 12 minutes, until lightly browned. Keep your eye on them because certain things like the peanut butter cups will definitely start exploding if overcooked.

Tiramisu StuffeD Portuguese Cookies

I first tried cookies like this at a Portuguese wedding. I loved the concept but found that most of the cookies were loaded with anise flavor on the inside, which isn't exactly my favorite, especially in desserts. I decided to make my own version with a tiramisu filling.

• •

MAKES: 20 COOKIES
HEAT: 0
PIG-OUT SCALE: 6.8

DOUGH

4 ounces (112 g) shortening

3½ cups (420 g) flour

1 egg

½ cup (100 g) sugar

½ cup (120 ml) cold water

FILLING

8 ounces (225 g) ladyfinger cookies, crushed

8 ounces (225 g) mascarpone cheese

1 cup (235 ml) coffee-flavored liqueur

½ cup (100 g) sugar

¼ cup (30 g) cocoa powder

Pinch of salt

MAKE THE DOUGH: Combine the shortening with the flour using a pastry blender or food processor. Mix in the egg, sugar and cold water, blending in the water last and adding just enough as needed to bring the dough together. Knead the dough just enough to combine it, about 3 minutes. Let it rest in the refrigerator for at least 30 minutes.

MAKE THE FILLING: In a bowl or a food processor, process the filling ingredients until well combined. You want a fairly smooth mixture that is able to be formed into a ball and hold its shape.

STUFF IT!: Run the dough through a pasta roller at the thickest setting. Fold the dough over itself and repeat 3 to 5 times to knead and smooth the dough. Roll the dough thinner in increments until you reach the fourth thinnest setting. Cut your dough into circles and put a ball of the filling onto each circle. Fold the dough over the filling, forming a half-moon shape. Seal the dough with a dab of water around the edge. Cut the edge of the dough to form a uniform half-circle shape. Place on a baking sheet.

BAKE IT: Preheat the oven to 350°F (180°C, or gas mark 4). Bake the cookies for about 20 minutes. Allow to cool before serving.

Sfogliatelle

MAKES: 20 LARGE SFOGLIATELLE
HEAT: 0
PIG-OUT SCALE: 6.8

DOUGH

3 cups (360 g) flour, plus more for rolling

1 teaspoon salt

1 cup (235 ml) water

½ cup (112 g) unsalted butter, softened

½ cup (112 g) lard, softened

Sfogliatelle is a crispy and delicious Italian pastry that has layers and layers of a crunchy shell. They were my grandfather's favorite dessert. After he passed away, I really wanted to make this Italian delicacy at home. I knew it would be pretty tough, but I thought that with my mom and sisters' help we would be able to figure it out. After reading countless recipes and watching a bunch of YouTube videos, we were finally ready to give it a shot! Although it is still a fairly involved recipe with some advanced techniques, it was actually much easier than I had expected. It was a fun family project with delicious results, and I highly suggest anyone interested give it a try.

• •

MAKE THE DOUGH: Combine the flour and salt in a large bowl and mix in about three-fourths of the water to start. Begin to knead the dough with your hands and if it comes together, it's ready. If not, add a little more water and keep going. Divide the dough in half and knead each half by running it through your pasta machine at the largest setting, then folding it over onto itself and repeating 12 times. Put the doughs on top of each other and run it through the pasta roller, then fold it onto itself, and run it through one last time. Fold the dough a few times to make it more manageable, wrap it up, and put it into the fridge for anywhere from 2 to 8 hours.

THIN IT OUT: Beat the butter and lard together until light and fluffy. It will look like some sort of delicious frosting, but don't take a bite!!!

Divide the dough in half again and keep half of it in the fridge.

Now divide the half you will be working with in half. Take the first half and run it through the pasta roller on the largest setting. Continue running it through, getting one single notch narrower on the machine each time, until you reach the thinnest setting. Lay the dough flat on the table and repeat with the other piece.

Now begin stretching your dough to make it even thinner. Stretch it widthwise to make it about 9 to 10 inches (23 to 25.5 cm) wide the whole way down the strip. You should easily be able to see your hand through the dough.

Once you have completed both sheets of dough, use a brush in conjunction with a spoon and probably your fingers to rub every inch of the dough with a super-thin coating of the lard-butter. Start at one end, and tightly roll the dough into a tube so that you end up with a 9-inch (23-cm) long tube of dough. When you get to the end of the first sheet of dough, bring the rolled tube to the end of the second sheet and continue rolling. Wrap the log in plastic wrap and put it into the fridge. Repeat with the second half of the dough. The hard work is now behind you! Let this sit in the fridge for another 2 hours. Also put the remaining lard-butter mixture into the fridge.

FILLING

⅔ cup (160 g) water

½ cup (100 g) sugar

½ cup (60 g) semolina flour

2 egg yolks

1 tablespoon (15 ml) vanilla extract

2 cups (450 g) ricotta cheese

1 tablespoon (15 ml) orange juice

1 tablespoon (6 g) orange zest

Pinch of cinnamon

Pinch of salt

MAKE THE FILLING: In a pot over high heat, bring the water and sugar to a boil, and whisk in the semolina. Cook until it becomes a paste and the semolina is tender, 2 to 5 minutes. Spread out on a plate and allow to cool for about 15 minutes.

Put the cooled semolina into a bowl and beat it a bit to break it up. Mix in the rest of the filling ingredients and beat until smooth.

FINALLY ... STUFF IT!: Line 2 baking sheets with parchment paper. Remove the remaining lard-butter from the fridge. Grab the two rolls from the fridge. Slice off as little as you can from the uneven edges. Cut ¾-inch (2 cm) rounds from the roll. Continue with the second roll. You should get about 10 slices from each roll.

Take each round and lay it flat on your work surface. This will seem weird, but flatten it out with your palm to make a 4-inch (10 cm) round, pressing out from the center. Now take the round in your hand and push the center down to form a cone shape that looks like a wizard's hat. You will notice the layers that you worked so hard to form are slightly separating as you do this, which is a good thing. Put in 2 to 3 tablespoons (30 to 45 g) of the filling mixture. Seal up the pastry at the bottom. Lay your pastries on the baking sheets and brush very lightly with the lard-butter.

COOK IT: Preheat the oven to 400°F (200°C, or gas mark 6). Bake the pastries for about 30 minutes, until crispy and browned. Serve ASAP, as these taste the best by far when they are fresh out of the oven.

Peach Habanero Stuffed Pizzelles

MAKES: 20 STUFFED PIZZELLES
HEAT: 4.8
PIG-OUT SCALE: 6.3

A little heat in dessert never hurt anyone, except maybe for people who have zero tolerance for spicy food. The real key to this dessert is the candied habaneros. They have the initial taste and texture of a Sour Patch Kid, followed by a quick slap in the face.

CANDIED HABANEROS

10 habaneros
1 cup (200 g) sugar, plus more for coating
½ cup (120 ml) water
¼ cup (60 ml) light corn syrup

PIZZELLES

3 eggs
2 teaspoons baking powder
½ teaspoon almond extract
1 teaspoon vanilla extract
1¾ cups (210 g) flour
½ cup (112 g) butter
¾ cup (150 g) sugar

CHOCOLATE GANACHE

⅓ cup (80 ml) cream
11 ounces (310 g) milk chocolate
1½ teaspoons corn syrup

CREAM FILLING

2 ripe peaches
2 habaneros, seeds removed
1 cup (225 g) mascarpone
1 cup (225 g) cream cheese
¾ cup (150 g) powdered sugar
Heavy cream, as needed

MAKE THE CANDIED HABANEROS: Remove the seeds from the habaneros and slice them into thin matchsticks. Mix the sugar, water and corn syrup in a pot with a candy thermometer and put it on low heat until the sugar is melted. Add the habaneros to the pot and stir to combine. Turn the heat to medium-high and bring to the low end of a hard-ball stage, 250°F (120°C, or gas mark ½). Meanwhile, put the sugar reserved for coating onto a plate, covering the plate. Using a fork, grab a few strands of habanero at a time and move them to the coating sugar. Roll them around in the sugar and allow to cool and dry.

MAKE THE PIZZELLES: Preheat your pizzelle maker. Mix all of the pizzelle ingredients. Put 1 scant tablespoon (15 ml) of the pizzelle batter in each indentation on the pizzelle maker. Cook for about 3 minutes, depending on your pizzelle maker. Remove the pizzelles carefully and work quickly to shape them into tube shapes like a cannoli. They should firm up within minutes. Repeat to make 20 pizzelle tubes.

MAKE THE GANACHE: Combine the chocolate ganache ingredients in a double boiler and heat until just melted, stirring to blend. One by one, dip the pizzelle ends into the ganache, just so that the tips are coated. Allow excess chocolate to drip off. Let the pizzelles cool on a sheet of waxed paper.

MAKE THE FILLING: Peel and pit the peaches. Place the peaches, habaneros, mascarpone, cream cheese and sugar into a food processor and process until smooth. Add a splash of cream if the mixture is too thick. Spoon the filling into a piping bag.

STUFF IT!: Pipe the peach mixture into the pizzelles. In the center of each opening, place one single candied habanero, then garnish the plate with the remainder of the candies.

Giant Peanut Butter cup

The first time I made a recipe in a tart pan I quickly realized that the pan is shaped like a peanut butter cup. It was only a matter of time before I would use the pan to create one. To make sure it wouldn't be overly rich, I decided to use brownie as the bottom, a peanut butter frosting in the center, and a chocolate ganache on top. It was still pretty rich, but the people I ate it with had no problem finishing their slices.

MAKES: 10 SERVINGS
HEAT: 0
PIG-OUT SCALE: 9.7

BROWNIE

½ cup (112 g) butter

5 ounces (140 g) 60% dark chocolate chips

1 teaspoon good-quality instant coffee

2 eggs

¾ cup (150 g) sugar

1 teaspoon vanilla extract

½ teaspoon salt

½ cup (60 g) plus 1 tablespoon (8 g) flour

PEANUT BUTTER FROSTING

1 cup (260 g) creamy peanut butter

1 cup (120 g) confectioners' sugar

4 tablespoons (56 g) butter, softened

1 teaspoon vanilla extract

Pinch of salt

¼ cup (60 ml) cream

CHOCOLATE GANACHE

1 cup (235 ml) heavy cream

2 pounds (908 g) milk chocolate

1 tablespoon (15 ml) light corn syrup

MAKE THE BROWNIE: Preheat the oven to 325°F (170°C, or gas mark 3). Butter a 12-inch (30.5-cm) tart pan with a removable bottom.

In a double boiler, heat the butter, chocolate and coffee, stirring often, just until melted and smooth. Remove from the heat and allow to cool slightly. Whisk in the eggs, sugar, vanilla and salt. Stir in the flour with a spatula until the mixture comes together. Pour the brownie mixture into the tart pan. It is kind of a thick brownie, so use a spatula to spread the brownie evenly. Put the tart pan onto a baking sheet in case some of the batter drips out. Bake the brownies for about 18 minutes, until just set. Remove from the oven and let cool.

MAKE THE FROSTING: Combine the peanut butter, confectioners' sugar, butter, vanilla and salt in a stand mixer with a paddle attachment and beat until combined. Add the cream and beat until light and creamy.

MAKE THE CHOCOLATE GANACHE: Melt the ganache ingredients together in a double boiler. Stir to combine.

STUFF IT!: Re-grease the visible area of the tart pan above where the brownie is. Also cut the brownie away from the sides of the pan to make it easier to slice later. Spread the peanut butter frosting all over the brownie, but leave about 1 inch (2.5 cm) around the edges, and make sure it doesn't go higher than the sides of the pan. Pour the ganache over the peanut butter and let it drip down the sides and fill the pan up to the very top. Refrigerate the tart for 2 hours. Take it out of the fridge and gently try and lift the tart out using the pull-away bottom of the pan. If it doesn't come out, run a toothpick along the edge of the pan in certain areas that seem extra stuck.

CHAPTER 6:

Basics

Here are some recipes I reference throughout; use them wisely.

Carnitas

2 cups (470 ml) orange juice

15 sprigs cilantro

2 shallots

6 cloves garlic

1 tablespoon (6 g) chipotle powder

2 teaspoons black pepper

2 teaspoons cumin

Pinch of cinnamon

Pinch of cloves

2 teaspoons salt

5-pound (2270-g) pork shoulder (Boston butt), bone in

Blend the orange juice, cilantro, shallots, garlic, chipotle, black pepper, cumin, cinnamon, cloves and salt in a food processor. Pour over the pork in a bowl, cover with plastic wrap and marinade overnight in the fridge.

The next day, preheat the oven to 250°F (120°C, or gas mark ½). Dump the pork and marinade into an oven-safe pot, uncovered. If needed, add a little water so the liquid goes about one-fourth of the way up the side of the pork. Bake for about 6 hours, until browned on the outside and falling apart. Shred with two forks or your hands.

Makes 2½ pounds (1.13 kg)

Pico de Gallo

5 vine ripened tomatoes, diced

1 red onion, diced

20 cilantro sprigs, finely chopped

3 to 5 jalapeños, diced and seeds removed

1 clove garlic, grated

Juice of 2 limes

1 teaspoon salt

Mix all the ingredients together in a bowl and dig in!

Makes 3-4 cups (175-235 g)

SPICE BLENDS

A well-stocked spice cabinet is a must-have in my kitchen. Knowing how and when to use spices can take your food from bland to aromatic and complex. Sneaking in a pinch of the right secret spice can make your guests pause and wonder, *What is that awesome flavor I'm tasting?*

The main thing is *how*, not *when*. There is a big difference between overpaying for a couple ounces of ground cumin from the grocery store that will lose what little flavor it has in a month, and buying a huge sack of whole cumin from an Indian market and grinding it as needed. I highly recommend buying all your spices whole and in large amounts from either ethnic markets or online. Keep a designated coffee grinder used only for grinding spices. Doing this will save you money and keep your spices fresh and flavorful for when you are ready to use them.

To make these recipes, first toast the whole spices in a dry frying pan, then grind in a spice grinder. Add any pre-ground spices like smoked paprika or turmeric after.

All-Purpose Curry Powder

1 tablespoon (6 g) fenugreek

1 tablespoon (11 g) black mustard seed

1 tablespoon (6 g) cumin

1 tablespoon (6 g) coriander

1 tablespoon (6 g) cardamom

1 teaspoon cloves, ground

1 teaspoon black pepper

1 teaspoon allspice

1-inch (2.5-cm) piece cinnamon

10 dried arbol chiles

2 teaspoons turmeric

All-Purpose Taco Seasoning

5 ancho chiles

5 chipotle chiles

2 tablespoons (30 g) brown sugar

2 tablespoons (12 g) cumin seed

1 tablespoon (18 g) salt

1 tablespoon (6 g) oregano

1 tablespoon (6 g) coriander

1 teaspoon black peppercorns

1 teaspoon mustard seed

½ teaspoon allspice

HEAD OF THE SHOP

The Moroccan spice blend ras el hanout literally translates to "head of the shop," or basically, the best spices that particular spice merchant has to offer. It commonly includes cardamom, coriander, cumin, clove and lots of other spices that I love and use often. I like to make my own ras el hanout, and always have it ready for a lazy night of cooking that just needs a little spice boost. Any time I make a curry powder, spice rub, or anything involving grinding spices, if I use less in the recipe than what I grind, I add the extra spices to a jar in my cabinet and give it a nice shake. It tastes a little different every time, but I know it is always the head of my shop.

Fresh Pasta Dough

4½ cups (540 g) flour

6 eggs

1 tablespoon (15 ml) olive oil

1 teaspoon salt

TRADITIONAL WAY: On a clean counter, make a pile of the flour with a crater in the center, just like when you are a kid and you make a space for gravy in your mashed potatoes. Crack your eggs into the center of the flour. With a fork, break the yolks and beat the eggs, slowly adding more and more flour to the mixture. Finally, get your hands involved, adding only as much flour as the dough seems to want to take in. In the end, most of the flour will be incorporated. Wrap the dough with plastic wrap and let it sit in the fridge for 30 minutes.

QUICK WAY: Put all the ingredients into a food processor and pulse until it comes together. Wrap the dough with plastic wrap and let sit in the fridge for 30 minutes.

WHAT'S NEXT?: Use the dough as the recipe directs. However, keep in mind that the dough needs a fair amount of kneading. When you begin to run it through the pasta roller, before you start thinning it out, run it through at the thickest setting, then fold it over and repeat. After doing this 3 to 5 times you will notice that the dough will become much smoother and more workable.

Makes 2 pounds (900 g)

Meaty Tomato Sauce

½ cup (120 ml) olive oil

½ pound (225 g) ground beef

Salt and pepper

2 medium white onions, diced

7 cloves garlic, minced

1 ½ (12-ounce [336-g]) cans tomato paste

5 (28-ounce [784-g]) cans crushed tomatoes

3 cups (705 ml) water

½ bunch basil, finely chopped

⅓ cup (20 g) finely chopped oregano

½ cup (50 g) grated Parmesan cheese

½ teaspoon sugar

¼ cup (60 ml) red wine

Crushed red pepper flakes, to taste

Get the olive oil into a large heavy-bottomed stockpot over high heat. Season the beef with salt and pepper and cook it until browned, about 10 minutes. Turn the heat to medium, remove the beef from the pot, drain out most of the fat and add the onions. Cook to sweat and reduce in size, but not quite brown, about 15 minutes. Add the garlic and cook for 2 minutes. Add the tomato paste and cook for another 3 to 4 minutes while stirring constantly. Dump in the crushed tomatoes, followed by all of the remaining ingredients, seasoning to taste and only adding enough water to achieve the desired consistency. Cover the pot but leave the cover a bit ajar. Bring to a simmer and turn to low, allowing the sauce to gently bubble away on the stove top for at least 2 hours.

Freeze what you don't use in separate serving-size containers.

Makes about 2 gallons (7.5 L) of sauce

Simple Marinara

¼ cup (60 ml) olive oil

2 cloves garlic, minced

2 tablespoons (20 g) minced onion

1 teaspoon dried oregano

Salt and pepper

1 (28-ounce [784-g]) can crushed tomatoes

Heat the olive oil in a skillet over medium heat. Add the garlic and onion and cook for 2 minutes. Add the oregano, salt and pepper and stir to combine. Add the crushed tomatoes and simmer for 15 minutes.

Makes about 3 cups (700 ml)

Pizza Dough

5 cups (600 g) flour, chilled, plus more for dusting

1 tablespoon (12 g) instant yeast

1 tablespoon (18 g) salt

1 ½ cups (355 ml) cold water

In a large mixing bowl, combine 2½ cups (300 g) of the flour with the yeast and salt, then add the water and stir well with a wooden spoon for about 3 minutes. Put this mixture into the fridge for 30 minutes. Mix in the remaining 2½ cups (300 g) flour.

On a floured surface (or in the bowl of a stand mixer fitted with the dough hook), knead the dough for about 15 minutes until smooth.

Let the dough rest in the fridge overnight. Remove from the fridge 1 hour before using. This can also be frozen BEFORE the overnight rest step. To defrost, remove from freezer and let sit in the fridge at least 36 hours.

Makes enough for 2 to 4 pizzas or 1 to 2 calzones

Basil-Carrot Raita

1 clove garlic, grated with a microplane

3 carrots, grated with a microplane

10 basil leaves

Juice of 1 lemon

1½ cups (340 g) Greek yogurt

½ teaspoon salt

Mix all the ingredients until combined. Allow to sit for 30 minutes before serving.

Makes 2 cups (450 g)

Thai Sweet and Sour Sauce

¼ cup (60 ml) agave

¼ cup (60 ml) lime juice

1 tablespoon (15 ml) rice wine vinegar

1 tablespoon (15 ml) Sriracha

1 teaspoon fish sauce

Pinch of salt

1 tablespoon (4 g) red pepper flakes

Mix all the ingredients until combined.

Makes ½ cup (120 ml)

Cream Sauce

¼ cup (57 g) butter

2 cloves garlic, grated

¼ cup (24 g) flour

2 cups (473 ml) light cream

4 cups (946 ml) whole milk

1 cup (179 g) Pecorino Romano

Melt the butter, then add the garlic. Cook about a minute. Now add the flour and whisk. Cook about 2 minutes until the color darkens slightly. Add the milk and cream and whisk. Bring to a simmer whisking the whole time. You will see the sauce slightly thicken as it comes to a simmer. Remove from heat and allow to cool a bit. Add in the cheese.

Makes about 6 cups (1.4 L)

Acknowledgments

Thanks to Will Kiester, Marissa Giambelluca and everyone at Page Street for helping shape my ramblings into something that actually resembles a coherent cookbook. Thanks to Sally Ekus for always having my back.

Thanks to Jim, Debbie, Mike, Shana, Mehera, Hana, Sergio, Greg, Nelson, Anna and everyone at Cafe Burrito for picking up the slack while I was working on this book. Thanks to Nate and Erin at tablespoon.com for all the ignored missed deadlines.

Thanks to my recipe testers, both casual recipe testers like Bianca (www.confessionsofachocoholic.com), Kathy (www.kathycancook.com), Jacki (www.justaddcheese.com), Rachel (http://forkitoverboston.blogspot.com), Steph, John, Fiona, Sal and Liz, and the real heavy hitters like Rich, Kim, Mom and Dad, Allie and Megan (http://megan-deliciousdishings.blogspot.com).

Thanks to anyone who has helped me with the blog over the years. To Sal and Nick, who chased away the viruses, Kim and Rich for the awesome artwork and design, and everyone who came to the pig roasts and beach parties. To John, Steph, my parents and anyone else who has allowed me to commandeer their kitchen and make a huge mess. Joanna, for always reminding me that I'm not as cool as I think. Thanks to anyone who has eaten something I made that was disgusting, knowing that it was in the name of discovery and science. Thanks to my rival and friend Nick at Macheesmo.com for always giving me a reason to strive to be better.

Thanks to my family for always supporting my drastic career decisions.

And thank you to Mandi, for always egging me on, being my biggest cheerleader and critic at the same time and forever the olive in my empanada.

About the Author

Dan Whalen is the founder and creator of the popular recipe blog The Food in My Beard. In the past four years since the website's inception, he has published more than 700 recipes that have been viewed more than 6 million times. He has been featured in many prestigious publications, such as *Saveur, Bon Appetit, Serious Eats, Fine Cooking,* Boston.com, MSNBC, and *Huffington Post.*

He currently lives in Boston, where he is writing for the General Mills blog, tablespoon.com. He also does restaurant menu consulting, the most recent of which was for a new burrito and coffee shop called Cafe Burrito in Belmont, Massachusetts. Belmont is also home to the artisan Gelato company where he worked for the past two years creating and developing new flavor combinations like Cucumber Lemon, Lucky Charms Cereal Milk, and Honey Corn.

When not working, Dan can usually be found looking for inspiration at indie rock shows, watching scripted TV series, eating out with his friends or playing Super Mario.

Index